A LILY IN LITTLE INDIA

A Comedy

by

DONALD HOWARTH

SAMUEL   FRENCH

LONDON

NEW YORK   TORONTO   SYDNEY   HOLLYWOOD

A LILY IN LITTLE INDIA

First presented by the Hampstead Theatre Club on the 22nd November 1965, and subsequently produced by Michael Codron by arrangement with Peterbridge Plays Limited, at the St Martin's Theatre, London, on the 20th January 1966, with the following cast of characters:

(in the order of their appearance)

GEORGE BLAND, a postman	*Ken Jones*
ANNA BOWERS	*Jill Bennett*
JACOB BOWERS, her father	*Leslie Handford*
MRS HANKER	*Jessie Evans*
ALVIN HANKER, her son	*Ian McKellen*
AMBULANCE MAN	*David Cook*
DOCTOR	*Raymond Mason*
AUTHOR'S VOICE	*Vernon Dobtcheff*

Directed by DONALD HOWARTH
Designed by KENNETH MELLOR

SYNOPSIS OF SCENES

The action of the play passes in the Hankers' and Bowers' houses and in the surrounding neighbourhood of a small, North-country town

ACT I
A morning in winter

ACT II
Later the same evening
(*The lights* BLACK-OUT *during Act II to denote the passing of two months*)

ACT III
A day or two later. Evening
(*The lights* BLACK-OUT *during Act III to denote the passing of some few weeks*)

Time—the present

ACT I

SCENE—*The Hankers' and Bowers' homes in a small, North-country town. A morning in winter.*

The stage is divided into two unequal areas. The larger area, R, represents the Hankers' house, the smaller area L, the Bowers'. Although doors are referred to in the text and dialogue, there is only one actual door on the stage, that leading into Alvin's room. This door has a practical lock. The other doors are indicated during the action by the response of the actor, who either looks up and towards the entrance as a character enters or leaves; by raising his voice and calling if a character is in another part of the house; i.e. one in the kitchen and the other in the hall, or by clearly moving precisely through the space where the door is supposed to be and changing direction consciously when the doorway has been passed through. On no occasion should the opening and closing of non-existent doors be mimed. For example, when Mrs Hanker goes from the kitchen into the hall to open the front door to Mr Bland, the actress should approach the entrance without looking at him and only when she is standing in front of him should she indicate that the barrier of the door has gone by looking at him and giving expression to recognition. Similarly, Mr Bland should look up at Mrs Hanker to coincide with her position in front of him on the door mat. When Anna closes the greenhouse door in the last act, she does so by moving away from up centre, waiting a moment and returning. The Bowers' house L, is on two levels. The main area, representing the living-room is on a rostrum eighteen inches high, with a smaller area, two feet higher at the back, to represent Jacob's bedroom. The entrance hall is up L. The Hankers' house R is on three levels, the kitchen and hall being on a rostrum six inches high. Stairs down R, in the hall, lead up to the landing, three feet six inches high, with George's bedroom slightly higher R of the landing and Mrs Hanker's bedroom slightly lower L of the landing. Two steps at the upstage end of the landing lead into Alvin's room. The area between and in front of the rostrums represents the outside world, the library, the field and the churchyard being played across the front and down C. The stage level and the sides of the rostrums are black to suggest a limbo area. Down LC at the front is a small box open on the upstage side, also painted black. This unit represents the field, the library steps and the grave. The library shelves are presumed to be in the fourth wall. There are two windows, one in the upstage wall of Alvin's room and one in the upstage wall of Jacob's room. In the Bowers' house L, the living-room has a sewing-table down R, a magazine rack down L, an upright chair at the sewing-table and a wheelchair up R. A dressmaker's dummy is L and there is a hatstand in the hall up L. In Jacob's room there is a single bedstead, a bedside table and an upright chair. A folding screen stands at the foot of the bed. In the Hankers' *house* R *the kitchen has a gas stove up* L *with a sink and a draining-board with a cupboard under it, below the stove. A small table down* L *has a radio standing on it. There is an armchair, facing front,* R *of this table. There is a kitchen table* R *with stools above and below it. A garbage bucket stands above the stove. In the hall down* R *there is a hall-table and a coat-stand. George's room, up* R, *has a single bed and an upright chair. Mrs Hanker's room has a single bed and a bedside table with a table-lamp on it. In Alvin's room there is a wardrobe up* R, *a chest of drawers* L, *a wicker armchair at the window and a stool below the chest of drawers. On the stage level,* R *of the rostrums, is a dustbin and a full bottle of milk. There are shaded pendant lights* R, RC, C, *and* LC.

When the CURTAIN *rises, the stage is in darkness.* GEORGE BLAND *is in bed. He is a postman and a lodger in Mrs Hanker's house. He is well set up all over. He is considered by the wives of the district to be "a bit of all right". A conformer, he is jealous of his independence and is an "I don't know-er" on questionnaires.* ALVIN HANKER *is out of sight behind the door of his bedroom. He is not bad to look at. Neither here nor there. He thinks without acting and vice versa.* JACOB BOWERS *is asleep in his bed up* L. *He is as old and forgetful as remembered childhood. Incapable. Pleading. White-haired. Resigned. He is an ex-Protestant minister and a dead bigot.* ANNA BOWERS *is standing down* L, *carrying a tray of breakfast for one. She is weak as hate, bitter, strained and sensual.* MRS HANKER *is out of sight up* C. *She is a widow, cuddly and unloved. She is deeply attached to Alvin, her only child. She is funny to watch, funny to hear. Sad, too. The sound of a clock ticking is heard through the loud-speakers.* GEORGE *snores. The alarm clock on the floor beside his bed rings.* GEORGE *wakes with a start, picks up the clock and hits it but the clock continues to ring.* GEORGE *sits up in bed and again hits the clock. It stops ringing.*

GEORGE. Five o'clock already? Some clocks have nothing better to do but tick all day. I'm glad I'm not a clock, though. At least that's something to be glad of. I'm not a clock. (*He gets out of bed*) I'm not wound or set the night before. I can get up in the morning when the alarm goes off. (*He puts his feet into his slippers, rises and puts the clock on the chair*) Nobody winds me. I'm not wound. Nobody has to wind me up to get me up.

(GEORGE *picks up his shirt from the chair, yawns, stretches and exits up* C. *The sound of the clock ticking stops. The lights come up on the living-room of the Bowers' house* L *and fade in George's room.*

ANNA, *carrying the tray, goes into Jacob's room. She puts the tray on the chair and opens the window curtains. The lights come up on Jacob's room.* ANNA *goes to the bedside table, opens a tin of Andrews Salts, puts a spoonful into a glass, pours water in from a jug and stirs it*)

ANNA. Father.

(JACOB *opens his eyes*)

JACOB. Wednesday?

ANNA. Yes, Wednesday.

(*A clock chimes the half-hour*)

Half past seven. Sit up.

(JACOB *eases his body out from under the snowdrift sheets, a frost-bitten explorer imagining rescue, and sits up.* ANNA *gives the glass to Jacob, goes to the tray and collects a table napkin.* JACOB *drinks the salts.* ANNA *returns to the bedside, tucks the napkin under Jacob's chin, takes the empty glass from him and puts it on the bedside table. She props Jacob up in bed, then goes to the chair for the tray.* JACOB *throws the napkin on to the floor.* ANNA *picks it up and tucks it in again, then gets the tray and places it on the bed in front of Jacob, then sits on the side of the bed and slices the top from Jacob's egg*)

It's likely to rain later today. Will you be getting up?

(JACOB, *after a moment's pause looks up at Anna*)

JACOB. Yes, I'll get up

(ANNA *pours a cup of tea for Jacob, then takes a spoonful of egg and hands it to* JACOB, *who dribbles it.* ANNA *rises, bends over Jacob and wipes his chin. She then sits on the chair beside the window.* JACOB *eats his breakfast. The lights dim on Jacob's room and the living-room* L *and come up on the Hankers' kitchen and Alvin's room. Music is heard from the radio in the kitchen.*

ALVIN *appears in his bedroom, putting on his overalls.*

MRS HANKER *enters up* C, *through the back door and comes into the kitchen. She picks up the garbage bucket above the stove and goes into the hall*)

MRS HANKER (*calling*) Alvin. (*She goes out of the front door, round the right side of the house to the dustbin and empties the garbage, then collects the bottle of milk outside the front door, goes into the kitchen, puts the bottle on the table, replaces the garbage bucket above the stove, then calls again*) Alvin. (*She goes to the table and pours milk from the bottle on to a plate of cereal*)

(ALVIN *leaves his bedroom, come slowly downstairs and blearily buttons up his overalls on the way. He goes into the kitchen, sits on the stool below the kitchen table and listlessly eats his cereal. The lights fade on Alvin's room*)

About time. (*She moves to the sink and washes up some dirty crockery*)

ALVIN. What is?

MRS HANKER. You are.

ALVIN. I always am.

MRS HANKER. George never is.

ALVIN. What?

MRS HANKER. Late.

ALVIN. I'm not.

MRS HANKER. You can tell the time by George Bland.

ALVIN. Who wants to at five o'clock in the morning?

MRS HANKER. Those who have a mind to. He's always on time is George Bland. He's never late. He's the first to leave this house regular as a clockwork at half past five every morning on the dot.

ALVIN. On his bicycle.

MRS HANKER. On the dot, five-thirty every morning.

ALVIN. Except Sunday.

MRS HANKER. Of course except Sunday. Nobody works on a Sunday.

ALVIN. A lot works on a Sunday.

MRS HANKER. Yes, but the majority don't. You know very well what I mean, very well you know it. (*She moves to the table*) As a postman Mister Bland's in the majority. (*She snatches Alvin's empty cereal plate and plunges it into the sink*) Awkward . . .

ALVIN (*taking some bread and butter*) I'm not being awkward.

MRS HANKER. Yes, y'are.

ALVIN. No, I'm not awkward.

MRS HANKER. You sound awkward.

ALVIN. I'm not, though.

MRS HANKER. I believe you. (*To herself*) Every morning except Sunday he leaves this house on his cycle regular as clockwork.

ALVIN. What time is it?

MRS HANKER (*pouring herself a mug of tea*) You're late.

ALVIN. I didn't ask if I was late.

MRS HANKER. You're always late.

ALVIN. I said what time is it?

MRS HANKER. I heard you.

ALVIN. Is it eight o'clock yet?

MRS HANKER. George Bland's never late.

ALVIN. Is it eight?

(MRS HANKER *suddenly puts her face close to Alvin's and shouts*)

MRS HANKER. You've got eyes, use 'em. (*She sits in the armchair and sips her tea*)

ALVIN (*rising and moving to the stove*) I'm late. (*He picks up the clock from the plate rack and stares crossly at it*)

MRS HANKER. I told you.

ALVIN (*replacing the clock and dashing into the hall*) I'm off. (*He frantically puts on his shoes, balaclava and donkey jacket*)

MRS HANKER. You've missed this bus and you won't catch the next.

ALVIN. I'll get the one after.

MRS HANKER. It'll be full.

ALVIN. I'll get it.

MRS HANKER. The one after's always full. You have to be at the head of the queue for the one after. You know as well as I or anybody. You have to get there first.

ALVIN. I can stand.

Mrs Hanker. George Bland's never late.

Alvin. He has a bicycle.

Mrs Hanker. I bet he's never stood on the one after.

Alvin. He has a bike . . .

Mrs Hanker. You'd still be last at the last push if you had a bike.

(Alvin *dashes into the kitchen, snatches a thermos and sandwich box from the table and grabs the remaining bread and butter*)

Announcer (*through the radio*) The time is eight-fifteen.

Mrs Hanker. The time is eight-fifteen.

Alvin. Ta-ra.

(Alvin *runs out of the kitchen and exits up* c)

Mrs Hanker. Always at the last push up. He'd never stand, wouldn't George. If George Bland went to work by bus instead of bike he'd get a seat. He'd be there first. He'd see to that. He wouldn't be at last push up.

(George *rides his bike from up* R *to down* R, *ringing his bell*)

(*She rises and puts her mug on the table*) Oh-ha-hergh-ha-he he is silly.

(George *dismounts, parks his bicycle down* R, *removes his hat, smooths his hair and replaces his hat. Simultaneously*, Mrs Hanker *comes into the hall, removes a curler from the front of her hair, preens herself in the imaginary mirror down* R, *puts the curler in the pocket of her slacks and goes to the door*)

(*She giggles*) Now, Mister Bland, what's all this? Why didn't you use your key?

George (*officially*) Does Alvin Hanker live here?

Mrs Hanker. You are silly.

George. There's a registered for him.

Mrs Hanker. Come in, daft.

George. Would you sign it, please?

Mrs Hanker. I haven't got a pencil.

George. I have.

Mrs Hanker. Sign it, then.

George. It wouldn't look right. Go on.

Mrs Hanker. Where? (*She takes the stub of pencil, the letter with the receipt and signs it*) Christian names?

George. No need.

Mrs Hanker (*writing*) Ivy Harriet Hanker. (*She hands the receipt to George*) Nothing for me?

George. No.

Mrs Hanker. Anything for you?

George. No.

Mrs Hanker. What's this for Alvin?

George. Can't I come in?

Mrs Hanker. What is it, do you think?

GEORGE. Is says on.

MRS HANKER (*reading from the back of the envelope*) "*Hockton Weekly News*". He couldn't have won the criss-crossword puzzle without telling me.

GEORGE. No.

MRS HANKER. If you'd been a minute sooner he was here. I could have asked him and found out. Aren't you coming in this morning? There's tea already made—he's only just this minute gone.

(GEORGE *crosses below Mrs Hanker, goes into the hall, puts his hat on the hall table and his postbag beside it on the floor.* MRS HANKER *peers at the registered letter*)

GEORGE. Open it. (*He goes into the kitchen, sits on the downstage stool and puts his packet of letters on the table*)

MRS HANKER. I would, but it's registered. I've signed for it. I can't open it as well. Takes all the pleasure out of getting it if it's opened *and* signed for. He'll get it tonight. (*She puts the letter on the hall table then goes into the kitchen*)

ANNOUNCER (*through the radio*) The time is eight-twenty. Twenty min . . .

(MRS HANKER *switches off the radio, goes to the stove and pours a mug of tea for George*)

GEORGE (*sorting the letters on the table*) I don't have so very many this morning.

MRS HANKER. I see. That's a lovely stamp.

(ANNA, *in the dim light, rises, places Jacob's dressing-gown on the bed within his reach, moves his tray to the end of the bed and comes into the living-room, pausing for a moment on the stairs with her hand on the newel post*)

GEORGE. By air for Miss Bowers on Stroggen Hill Road.

MRS HANKER. What country is it? (*She puts George's tea on the table beside him*) Your tea.

GEORGE. Ceylon.

MRS HANKER. Oh, lovely. Slice of bread?

GEORGE. No.

MRS HANKER. Anna Bowers, "Byeways", Stroggen Hill Road, Hockton, England. Lovely.

(ANNA *goes to the sewing-table, takes a box of pins out of the bucket drawer, goes to the dressmaker's dummy, kneels, puts the pins on the floor beside her and pins up the hem of the dress*)

Any postcards today?

GEORGE. There's one with a joke.

MRS HANKER. Have you read it?

GEORGE. I saw the picture.

MRS HANKER. What does it say? (*She sits on the upstage stool*)

GEORGE. Read it. (*He hands the card to Mrs Hanker*)

MRS HANKER (*laughing*) Ohohi-haa-ha-he-ah. (*She reads*) "Mister, can I borrow your rubber mattress? That's not a rubber mattress, that's my wife in a bathing suit." (*She laughs alone*) Ooerhha. You have to look at it to get the funny side. Here. (*She returns the card to George and rises*) I don't know how they dare print them.

GEORGE. I've seen worse.

MRS HANKER (*standing between the table and sink, facing down stage and striking a pose*) I hope I never get as fat as that.

GEORGE. No, you're not that kind.

MRS HANKER. How do you know?

GEORGE. I'm a fairly good judge.

MRS HANKER. Are you?

GEORGE. I can tell if a woman's going to run to fat or not. You'll stay as you are for a long time yet.

MRS HANKER. You think so.

GEORGE. There's plenty of wear left in you for that. A good ten years, I'd say.

MRS HANKER. You make me sound like a second-hand carpet.

GEORGE. I didn't mean to.

MRS HANKER. I should hope not. I don't let anybody walk over me.

GEORGE. I know that.

MRS HANKER. Nobody wipes their feet on Ivy Hanker.

GEORGE. Unless they take their shoes off first. (*He drinks his mug of tea in one slow draught, looking at Mrs Hanker all the time*)

(MRS HANKER *watches* GEORGE *all the time as well. He finishes the tea, takes the mug from his lips and hands it slowly to* MRS HANKER. *She takes it like a bad Carmen, sits on the right arm of the armchair and looks into the mug*)

MRS HANKER. I'll tell your fortune for you one of these days.

GEORGE. I can guess what it'll be.

MRS HANKER. I bet you don't.

GEORGE. I've a good idea.

MRS HANKER (*reading the tea leaves*) Oh! I say!

GEORGE. What?

MRS HANKER. My goodness me!

GEORGE. What is it?

MRS HANKER. Well, I never!

GEORGE. Eh?

MRS HANKER. Fancy that now.

GEORGE. Is it bad?

MRS HANKER. That is interesting.

GEORGE. Is it good?

MRS HANKER. My word, it is a big one.

GEORGE. What?

MRS HANKER. Very big.

GEORGE. What is?

MRS HANKER. It's all there, all right, crystal clear, cut and dried

GEORGE (*rising and moving to* R *of Mrs Hanker*) Let me see.

MRS HANKER (*rising and moving to the sink*) I wouldn't dream . . .

GEORGE. Why not?

MRS HANKER. I wouldn't know where to look. (*She plunges the mug into the sink and swills it out*)

(GEORGE *collects his letters from the table.* MRS HANKER *crosses below George and goes into the hall.* GEORGE *follows and grabs his hat from the hall table, whilst* MRS HANKER *bends down and picks up his post bag*)

Have you got your letters?

GEORGE. Yes. (*He goes to the door and steps outside*)

MRS HANKER (*handing him the post bag*) Watch yourself.

GEORGE. You watch yourself.

MRS HANKER. I'm watching you.

GEORGE. Keep your eyes skinned, then.

MRS HANKER. Let me know if I miss anything.

GEORGE. I'll make sure you don't.

MRS HANKER. Cheeky devil.

GEORGE (*looking up*) Weather doesn't look very promising. I bet I get my feet wet.

MRS HANKER. Looks like we're in for a spot of rain.

GEORGE. I'll get my feet wet, I bet.

MRS HANKER. Then you'll have to take your shoes off when you come home.

(GEORGE *goes to his bicycle and "freezes" his position, as does* ANNA *at her dummy. The lights come up in George's room*)

(*She goes into George's bedroom and makes his bed. She illustrates her speech with the folding of his pyjamas*) A walking man like George, never-late George, a man who rides a bike when he doesn't walk, he must have legs as heavy as pistons, calves as thick as thighs and lungs to breathe with. A pair of lungs locked away in a rib cage wider than Uncle Jack's. He carries a bag on a shoulder, too and that's not empty. He's a forward man. Too much of it. Have a joke and he walks a mile. I'll take his shoes off and tickle his toes. He needs a peg or two taking out; too big for his boots by half a size. I'll have to be careful before I like him any more. If I've got to like him I'd better not show it.

(GEORGE *"unfreezes"*)

He should wear rubbers when it rains, I've told him before. (*She "freezes" her position in George's bedroom*)

GEORGE. She's definitely pushing. She's certainly leading me on. She's almost too willing. Too eager, too. Too soon in some ways, if you like. (*He wheels his bicycle a short distance* c) Women are all right, but she has no manners with her; no proportion of when to stop going too far. I like to coax a woman. Fondle her fancy with a joke or a smile then try a bit more till some months later, I know that I'm liked. When liking's achieved a man's confidence grows and who knows where that might lead to from there? A confident man who's liked—he's a valuable thing not easy to come by nor to meet with. Confidence can't be got quickly. A man needs time. She's too willing too soon, I think. Too eager. Putting me off, pushing me, leading me on. (*He looks upwards*) If it rains I should wear goloshes. (*He gets on his bicycle and rides across the front of the stage to the Bowers' house*)

> (*The lights dim on the Hankers' house and come up on the Bowers' house* l. Anna *and* Mrs Hanker *"unfreeze".* Mrs Hanker *finishes making George's bed.* Anna *rises, replaces the pins in the sewing-table and goes to the front door.* Jacob *gets out of bed and puts on his dressing-gown and slippers*)

(*He holds out a letter to Anna*) Air mail.
Anna (*taking the letter*) Thank you.
George. Ceylon.
Anna. Ceylon!

> (George *rides off up* l)

(*She moves down stage, faces front, opens her letter and reads it*) "Today's lesson is taken from Brother Maurice's epistle to St Anna of the Michaelmas Daisies, the only surviving Methodist nun west of Brighouse. Chapter six, verses one to eighteen—and after the monsoons came water in the swamps . . ." (*She moves and stands above the sewing-table and looks out of an imaginary window*) It can't rain in Ceylon. Not like it does here. Ceylon rain comes teeming, monsoonfuls at a time. Rain like that's as good as thunder. Nothing so good in Hockton. Nothing so much as a flash in the sky. Just grey rain every fortnight for a week. (*She goes to the sewing-table, sits at it, takes writing materials from the drawer, puts them on the table, and moves the vase of Michaelmas daisies from the centre of the table to the right end of it*)

> (Mrs Hanker *comes downstairs, puts her coat on at the hall-stand, picks up a shopping basket from under the hall table and exits down* r. *The lights fade on the Hankers' house* r. Jacob *reaches for his walking-stick and comes downstairs. Fade lights on Jacob's room*)

Jacob. Anna. Anna.
Anna. What do you want?
Jacob. Nothing.
Anna. Why did you call me?
Jacob. I was on my own.
Anna. You still are.

(JACOB *moves the wheel chair so that it is* L *of Anna and* R *of the magazine rack*)

JACOB. Writing a letter?

ANNA. Yes.

JACOB. To Aunt Milly?

ANNA. Yes, Aunt Milly.

JACOB. Send her my love.

ANNA. I will.

JACOB. I never get any replies to my letters.

ANNA. You never write any.

JACOB. I do.

ANNA. Postcards aren't letters. Nobody answers postcards.

JACOB (*sitting in the wheel chair*) Your brother Maurice, he never writes. I wonder where he is.

ANNA. We'll never know—he won't write here.

JACOB. Couldn't you write to his old address—to that shipping line he used to work for?

ANNA. You told me not to.

JACOB. Yes, but I'm older now. Seven years.

(ANNA "*freezes*" *Jacob with a look*)

ANNA. You're over seventy. (*She writes*) "My dear Maurice. Thank you for your letter which I received this morning. Ceylon sounds nice. I went for a walk last Sunday. The fish pond is frozen over. I still get plenty of sewing to do. I'm altering an afternoon frock at the moment for a fat customer. I do hate alterations. There's no satisfaction in alterations. Nothing exciting has happened . . ."

(*A clock chimes five*)

JACOB. Still raining?

ANNA. You woke up, then?

JACOB. Yes, I dozed off.

ANNA (*fingering the daisies in the vase*) These are dead, anyway, these daisies.

JACOB. What's the time?

ANNA. Five o'clock.

JACOB. Did the postman come this morning?

ANNA. No.

JACOB. I thought I heard him.

ANNA. Pamphlets, that's all.

JACOB. I wish Maurice would write sometimes. I like to know where he is—what he's doing.

ANNA. You must expect to be ignored.

JACOB. How he feels. How he's getting on in the world. It's natural.

ANNA. Selfish.

JACOB. Old people are selfish.

ANNA. They shouldn't be. You talk as though old age were a licence for feeble behaviour. It isn't.

JACOB. I'm his father.

ANNA. Don't talk any more.

JACOB. I'm getting old.

ANNA. Read tonight's paper. (*She opens the bucket of the sewing-table and takes out a magnifying glass*) It's there.

JACOB. I couldn't find last week's. (*He takes a newspaper from the magazine rack*)

ANNA. I threw it away. (*She breathes on the magnifying glass and polishes it with the edge of her jumper*)

JACOB. But I hadn't finished the crossword.

ANNA. There'll be a new one tomorrow.

JACOB. I like to check it over with the clues. It's natural.

ANNA (*holding out the glass to Jacob*) Selfish.

JACOB (*snatching the glass from her*) It's natural when a puzzle's part complete to check it over.

(ANNA "*freezes*" *while looking at her letter*)

Well over seventy. Over seventy clues. I did some across and I did some down. The easy years were filled in and there were others I couldn't attempt.

ANNA (*"unfreezing" and reading her letter*) "Our father, which art in Hockton, is sleeping."

JACOB. I'm feeble at all hours of the day.

ANNA. "He does all the time."

JACOB. I want to be ignored.

ANNA. "I'm sending you some cuttings from a local paper."

JACOB. She knew and threw it away or lit a fire with it on purpose.

ANNA. "The town is getting ready for the Flower Show although it's six months away. They've asked me to make baby clothes again for the White Elephant stall."

JACOB. I don't like her.

ANNA. Baby clothes.

JACOB. I never wanted a daughter.

ANNA. "I suppose I shall have to." (*She gathers her writing things together*)

JACOB. She's an ugly woman with a dead woman. *De Mortuis nil nisi bonum.*

ANNA. "Take care."

JACOB. She's a girl.

ANNA. "Look after yourself."

JACOB. I didn't want.

ANNA (*rising*) "Your ever loving sister of the Michaelmas Daisies." (*She takes the dead flowers from the vase*)

JACOB. I never liked.

ANNA. "Anna."

JACOB. I'm reading the paper if she looks.

(ANNA *picks up her writing things, goes into Jacob's room, puts the daisies on the breakfast tray and straightens the bed. She then sits in the chair by the window and continues writing her letter*)

They're writing about the Flower Show already, Anna.

(*The lights fade on the Bowers' house* L *and come up on the Hankers' house* R.

ALVIN *rushes on up* R, *goes into the hall and wipes his feet on the door mat. He sees the letter on the hall-table, picks it up, sits on the bottom stair, opens the letter and reads it.*

MRS HANKER *enters up* C, *through the back door and comes into the kitchen. She carries a basket of groceries. She removes her head scarf and puts it with the basket on the armchair, then goes into the hall*)

MRS HANKER. Well?

ALVIN. Well, what?

MRS HANKER. Tell us what?

ALVIN. Crossword prize, that's all.

MRS HANKER. What, first? (*She snatches the letter from Alvin*) First prize?

(ALVIN *snatches the letter from Mrs Hanker*)

Tell us.

ALVIN. No.

MRS HANKER. Ah, come on.

ALVIN. No.

MRS HANKER. Have you won?

ALVIN. No.

MRS HANKER. I could see you hadn't. (*She removes her coat and hangs it in the hall*)

ALVIN. Third prize.

MRS HANKER. I might have known. I might have known you'd be a runner-up. Trust you. (*She goes into the kitchen*)

ALVIN (*rising and following Mrs Hanker into the kitchen*) It's not my fault.

MRS HANKER. It never is.

ALVIN. I got it right.

MRS HANKER. Why didn't you win, then?

ALVIN. That one wins who gets his envelope opened first.

MRS HANKER (*taking the groceries from the basket and putting them into the cupboard beneath the draining-board*) And that one wins who gets his envelope first into the post. First arrived is first opened. You were allus a runner-up, allus were, allus will be. You're like your dad in that respect. You take after him. Late for his own funeral—died six weeks after they said he would. I knew he would. "You'll never make it," I said. "You won't see death this side of ten weeks never mind four," I told him and I was right. (*She becomes tearful*)

Late for his own deadline in spite of my warnings; all I tried to do.
You get it from your dad. (*She hands the empty basket to Alvin*)

(ALVIN *puts the basket under the hall table*)

ALVIN. Why drag him into it?

MRS HANKER. I don't want you to think you get it from your
mother, that's all.

ALVIN. Get what from you?

MRS HANKER. Don't pretend you don't know.

ALVIN (*moving into the kitchen*) I don't.

MRS HANKER. Yes, you do.

ALVIN. No.

MRS HANKER. And I say yes.

ALVIN. What for? (*He takes the thermos flask and sandwich box from
his coat pockets*)

MRS HANKER. I'll give you what for.

ALVIN. Why?

MRS HANKER. You could have won if you'd put your heart into
it. If once you'd knuckle under and get down to it I know you'd
come out on top. (*She takes the flask and box from Alvin and washes
them in the sink*) But you won't. At school you were bottom. Allus
bottom. Best dunce they ever had at Woodroyd Elementary.

(ALVIN *sits on the downstage stool, still holding his letter*)

When you *did* move up it was because of your age and even then
you weren't ashamed for a boy of your years. You never scored
goals in winter nor batted in June, you were a wash-out on Whit
Monday's sports.

ALVIN. I broke my ankle.

MRS HANKER. Running in a sack. You can neither swim nor ride
a bike, the army didn't want you, no girl'll have you, you lost all
your marbles, you broke the string on your kite—you're a failure.

ALVIN. I wish I hadn't sent it.

MRS HANKER. Then you'd be nowhere, that's where you like. A
nobody nowhere's where you'll end up. (*She washes up the dishes*)

ALVIN. When did you ever win anything?

MRS HANKER. I won you.

ALVIN. I wish you'd never.

MRS HANKER. May be.

ALVIN. Perhaps.

MRS HANKER. What do they give you for being third, anyway, is
it owt worth having?

(ALVIN *rises, rushes into the hall in a rage, rips off his jacket and hangs
it on the hall-stand*)

Alvin—you can come back here and close that door properly.

(ALVIN *goes up the stairs*)

B

(*She goes into the hall*) Do you hear me? (*She goes up the stairs*)

> (Alvin *goes into his room.*
>
> George *enters down* R *on his bicycle, gets off and parks the bicycle down* R)

I asked you what you get for being third prize?

> (Alvin *locks his door.* George *enters the hall and slams his hat down on the hall-table*)

(*She turns*) Mr Bland. You're home, are you?

George (*cheerily*) Hello. (*He removes his jacket and hangs it in the hall*)

Mrs Hanker (*coming downstairs*) Did you get wet?

George. Yes.

Mrs Hanker. Take your shoes off then before you tramp in there. (*She glares up at Alvin's door*)

George (*removing his shoes*) What's wrong with Alvin?

Mrs Hanker (*at the newel post*) Came third in last week's cross-word and sulks about it. He's a bad loser, that's all, like his dad. A bad loser. God, your feet smell! (*She crosses below George and goes into the kitchen*)

George. What's for tea?

Mrs Hanker. Wait and see. (*She collects George's slippers*)

George (*looking in the imaginary hall mirror*) I'm beginning to look old, ugly at the edges; if you look round the corners, into the crevices you can see it isn't youth like it used to be. Close looks reveals age and a little bit of ugliness. I hope nobody notices.

Mrs Hanker (*throwing George's slippers into the hall*) Wash your hands and feet before you eat.

George (*putting on his slippers*) She's very disapproving for tea-time. I can't smell my feet, and if I could I wouldn't bring them up in conversation. Most days I wash between the toes and nobody tells me to. Nobody tells me what to do.

> (George *goes to his room then exits up* C *to the bathroom.* Alvin *switches on his record player.* Mrs Hanker, *during the first verse of the music, takes George's tea from the cupboard under the draining-board and lays the table, drying up articles from the draining-board to do so.* Alvin *also during the first verse, removes his overall and hangs it behind the door of his room*)

Count to Ten

Verse 1

Number one has begun
Number two is all the way through
Number three, wait for me,
Four, close the door
Five, I'll survive
Six, no more tricks
Seven, till eleven

Eight, I can't wait
Nine, until you're mine
When you count to ten
Won't you tell me then
That you're gonna love me again.

(GEORGE *re-enters and goes into his bedroom during the interim music between verses. He is drying himself with his towel and jigs about to the music. At the same time,* MRS HANKER *starts to shout at* ALVIN *who tries to dance defiantly with his hands in his pockets.* MRS HANKER'S *following speech is simultaneous with the music of Verse 2*)

Verse 2

Number one having fun
Number two is my love for you
Number three, lucky me
Four I adore
Five being alive
Six, had my fix
Seven, I'm in heaven
Eight, make me wait
Nine and then be mine
Honey count to ten
One more time and then—
Say you're gonna love me again.

MRS HANKER. Alvin; Alvin, switch it off. Stop it. We don't want any more, understand? I'll break it over his empty head if he doesn't put its jacket on straightaway. (*She goes into the hall*) It's indecent at tea-time with the neighbours listening. Please, Alvin. You know I hate the hooligan jives and you jerking on the ceiling. (*She stands at the foot of the stairs and shouts*) Stop it or I'll bounce you one.

(ALVIN *turns up the volume*)

Are you hearing me? Do you listen? Mrs Raistrick'll be coming round again and not without reason, so stop it. (*She goes up the stairs*) I can't be bothered with her. George Bland doesn't like it, either— do you, Mr Bland?

GEORGE (*coming to his bedroom door*) Hello?

MRS HANKER (*changing her approach to one of demure frailty*) Mister Bland . . .

GEORGE. I'm listening.

(ALVIN *looks towards the door, turns down the volume, takes his stool to the door, stands on it and looks through the glass fanlight at George and Mrs Hanker*)

MRS HANKER. Then I wish you'd tell our Alvin what you think of him before you come down. He needs a man behind him to talk to him, to show him what's what and what it's for. And that's where you come in, Mister Bland. Show him what you're made of and ask him what does he think I feel while you're at it. A woman can't be doing it all the time alone.

(GEORGE *catches sight of Alvin and stares up at him*)

It needs a man, it needs you to tell him, George. (*She follows George's stare and moves to Alvin's door*)

(ALVIN *steps from the stool, replaces it, turns up the volume of the record player and sits in the chair by the window.*
GEORGE *exits up* C *to the bathroom*)

(*She tries Alvin's door, finds it locked and shouts through the keyhole*) If only you'd read a book all through for once or play cards—find yourself a hobby like other people have to or go out to the pictures —night school or Bert Shutt's dancing.

(ALVIN *covers his ears*)

Anything to get a move on out of my sight.

(ALVIN *snatches the pick-up off the record*)

ALVIN (*shouting*) Shut up!
MRS HANKER (*after a pause; quietly*) You shouldn't have spoken like that, Alvin, not to your mother.
ALVIN. Go away.
MRS HANKER. Mister Bland's here. Open this door. (*She bangs on the door*)
ALVIN. Stop it.
MRS HANKER (*having an imaginary conversation with George*) Mister Bland—belt him. Take your belt off and whack him. His father never would. (*To Alvin*) Open the door. He never had it. He never had a belting, that's why he needs it. You have my permission.
ALVIN (*kneeling behind the door*) You can't.
MRS HANKER. As you won't do what I say, Mister Bland's coming to show you how about it. He's going to belt you with his strap.
ALVIN. No.
MRS HANKER. It's "no", is it?
ALVIN. I'm sorry.
MRS HANKER. Too late for sorry now.
ALVIN. I won't play it any more.
MRS HANKER. You've said that before.
ALVIN. I won't say it again.
MRS HANKER. Mister Bland's going to make sure this time. He'll knock some sense through you with the buckle end. You'll knuckle under for him. He'll make you get down to it.
ALVIN. I'm sorry I was third. I won't be if you go away. I'll win if you leave me alone.

Mrs Hanker. Blackmail and threats won't make you top. Open up for Mister Bland.

Alvin. I promise I'll make you glad I'm Alvin. I will. In the name of our dad I'll be first prize-winner, the best there is for ever and ever after.

Mrs Hanker. We believe that.

Alvin. I promise you—I swear it.

Mrs Hanker. What on?

Alvin. My record. (*He crawls on his knees to the record player, removes the record, holds it up in the air and breaks it in pieces*) My disc, on my pop that you don't like—(*he crawls to the door and pushes the pieces under the door for Mrs Hanker to see*) here—here, you see.

Mrs Hanker. You're a lunatic.

Alvin. I'm Alvin Hanker.

Mrs Hanker (*looking down at the pieces*) I shan't sweep it up.

Alvin (*after a listening pause*) I'll beat the world. I'll find something. If you can wait I'll be at the front. You'll look up—if you don't hit me——

(George *enters from the bathroom, carrying his belt and putting on his pullover*)

—if you never use the buckle end.

George (*coming on to the landing*) I'm here. I'm ready.

Mrs Hanker (*pushing George to the stairs*) Come along then, George, and have your tea. Put your belt on.

(*They go down into the hall and pause at the bottom of the stairs*)

George. What about Alvin?

Mrs Hanker. Alvin's not worth bothering about. Fasten up and let's see what's on the table. I bet you're famished.

George. I could do with a bite.

Mrs Hanker. What of?

George. What I fancy.

Mrs Hanker. What's that?

George. What have you got?

Mrs Hanker. What you fancy.

George. What's that?

Mrs Hanker. It's all laid out on the table.

(*They go into the kitchen.* George *sits on the downstage stool*)

(*She takes the teapot from the stove, puts it on the table, then moves the upstage stool to* L *of the table and sits*) You can pick and choose where you like. Bread and butter plus a bit of tongue. Half a plate of pie and tomatoes with it if you want them, pineapple preserved while the custard's still warm and lemon curd with the pastry. You can wash it all down with a second cup of best Ceylon tea, fresh today. I bought it for you to like. Two and fourpence.

(*The lights fade on the kitchen, leaving only Alvin's room lit.* ALVIN, *still on his knees, opens his door, leans out, listens, picks up the pieces of record, then closes the door. Throughout the following speech,* MRS HANKER, GEORGE, ANNA *and* JACOB *are in a "freeze".* ALVIN, *still on his knees, tries to piece the record together*)

ALVIN. You're silenced for ever if your groove's not joined. I'm sorry I broke you in sacrifice. (*He rises and puts the pieces into the drawer of the chest of drawers*) Never mind. I'll get you another one again. (*He mimics his mother's voice*) "If only you'd read for once or play cards. Find yourself a hobby like other people, go to the pictures, the night school, the dancing, the football, the . . ." Night school. If I went to night school I'd be a student. Alvin student. There are too many. Students all trying. Besides, there's only one for the top of the class. I might look well with a hobby. If you have a private sideline, that's it. No-one expects you to present the result. (*He sits in the chair*) You can do it when you come home from work and you're all right at week-ends. I could dance. I could be taught. (*He mimics a young woman's voice*) "Bert Shutt's Palais's no good for dancing in with Alvin Hanker." (*He rises and takes an imaginary partner*) A dance floor's for partners. (*He dances*) Four legs behave as two on the ballroom boards. (*He steps on his partner's toes*) Never mind dancing. (*He sits*) Too many dance. Too many legs on ballroom floors, crowding each other out on to the pavements. Dancing's overcrowded like the pavements. All going to the pictures. I like the pictures. Sitting in the pictures—getting dark and warm and watching with the music all the time playing from nowhere. Film stars are real and all first class with big faces—and they're good at it. I get on well at the films. It would be sitting at the pictures if I could have the money to do it full time. I could borrow. But there's the travelling to get to the one the night after and seeing a different one every middle of the week. I couldn't afford the fares into town as well as a reasonable seat for sitting in. Playing at cards isn't for one, except patience. But I cheat so that's out. I could read. It's quiet. I could read a lot. Seven books a week. Library books. Long books—full of quiet reading far from Mrs Raistrick's ears. Books with photographs beside the print, beautiful, like film stars, but quiet. Slender, thin-backed books with titles, books on buildings, books on ships, on bridges, books on end, books on wardrobes never dusted, books on gardening books. Flower books on flowers. (*He backs himself up on the chair until he is standing on it, then he turns to the wardrobe and pushes off the old books, comics, etc., before picking up the gardening book. He mimics Mrs Hanker, standing on the chair, facing* L *and holding the book*)

"What's that, Alvin?"

A secret.

"A secret what?"

Hobby.

"Hobby what?"

(ALVIN *sits on the back of the chair with his feet on the seat*)

Just hobby.
"Come here."
No.
"Where're you going?"
To hobby.
(*Calling*) "Alvin . . ."

(ALVIN *slips on to the seat of the chair and sits curled up in it*)

I can't miss it.
"Hurry up, then."
I can't be late. I must get up. Mustn't forget.
"You won't."
"I can't."
"You shan't."
I haven't.

(*The lights come up on the kitchen. Tea is finished*)

MRS HANKER. You aren't going to tell me you didn't enjoy that
'cause I know you did.
GEORGE. A good tea.
MRS HANKER. Have some more tongue.
GEORGE. No more.
MRS HANKER. I'm putting it away.
GEORGE. I'm full.
MRS HANKER. You're sure.
GEORGE. I am.
MRS HANKER. Lemon curd?
GEORGE. No.
MRS HANKER (*picking up the teapot*) Or a third cup of tea?
GEORGE. Half a cup.
MRS HANKER. Hold it out under the spout.
GEORGE (*holding out his cup*) Don't fill it up.
MRS HANKER (*pouring tea into George's cup*) What are you doing
tonight?
GEORGE. I'll have a drink.
MRS HANKER. At the pub? (*She replaces the teapot*)
GEORGE. Or the club.
MRS HANKER (*with a swift change of mood*) I see. Sugar yourself.
(*She rises, pushes the stool under the table and commences to clear the crockery
into the sink*) I'll clear these and then I'll wash up.
GEORGE. I'll dry.
MRS HANKER. No, you won't.
GEORGE. Yes, I will.
MRS HANKER. You stay there.
GEORGE. I can help.

Mrs Hanker. Drink your tea.

George (*rising and moving to the sink*) Where's the cloth?

Mrs Hanker. Take your hook.

George (*picking up the teacloth*) Might as well—now I'm up.

Mrs Hanker (*snatching the cloth from him*) Sit you down.

George (*snatching the cloth from her*) Give it me.

Mrs Hanker (*snatching the cloth violently from him*) Do you hear what I say? (*She puts the cloth firmly on the draining-board as though challenging George to touch it again*)

George. What is it?

Mrs Hanker. What?

George. Wrong?

Mrs Hanker. Nowt.

George. Liar.

Mrs Hanker. It's my house.

George. So?

Mrs Hanker. I can lie if I want.

George. Why?

Mrs Hanker. Don't ask.

George (*moving R*) I've a right.

Mrs Hanker. Why?

George. I live here. (*He sits on the downstage stool, facing L*)

Mrs Hanker. When do you leave?

George (*alarmed*) Leave?

Mrs Hanker. Go then.

George. Where?

Mrs Hanker. Off out drinking?

George. It's that, is it?

Mrs Hanker. Three cups of tea and you're thirsty.

George. No.

Mrs Hanker (*returning to the sink and noisily washing up*) Boozing.

George. No.

Mrs Hanker (*throwing cutlery into the sink*) In the saloon.

George. No.

Mrs Hanker. Tippling.

George. No.

Mrs Hanker. Guzzling.

George. No. It's not the beer I go for.

Mrs Hanker (*turning sharply to him*) What, then?

George. I go for the noise.

Mrs Hanker (*moving menacingly to him*) Too quiet for you here?

George. Not a bit.

Mrs Hanker. It's Alvin puts you off.

George. Not a bit.

Mrs Hanker. Doesn't he?

George. No.

Mrs Hanker. Who then?

George (*after a pause*) That's right, he does.

Mrs Hanker (*moving to the sink*) I thought so. (*She washes some cutlery*) He's in your way.

George. He is a bit.

Mrs Hanker. You feel awkward with him in the house. (*She opens the kitchen drawer and dries cutlery into it during her speech*) I've noticed. You feel hemmed in, cooped up, tied hand and foot, he drives you out all the time, he puts you off what you're thinking. You should have complained, own it, come on, own up.

George. Well, yes, I do feel a bit awkward with him in the house.

Mrs Hanker. You can never be sure when he won't come in.

George. No.

Mrs Hanker. If he's listening somewhere or watching to catch you unawares.

George. You can't be sure.

Mrs Hanker. The walls are thin in these houses.

George. Pre-war.

Mrs Hanker. Mrs Raistrick listens, as well. No wonder you feel you have to go out every night. You can't keep your thoughts to yourself with Alvin behind the walls everywhere you look. How can you relax?

George. I don't feel comfortable when he's in.

Mrs Hanker. You'd stay if he weren't. You wouldn't go out if he were. (*She closes the drawer and goes to the sink*)

(George *shakes his head in agreement*)

George. I like the noise at the club, though, darts dropped on the board, piano tunes off and on and the till bell and the bitter glasses chinking as you count your change.

Mrs Hanker. But it's Alvin drives you to the bar—you're not tell me it's noise.

(Alvin *slams his book shut, rises, goes into the hall and puts on his scarf and balaclava. The lights come up on the Bowers' house L.* Anna *rises, goes downstairs, takes her coat and scarf from the hall-stand and puts them over the back of the chair. She puts her letter on the seat of the chair and her writing things into the sewing-table drawer. She then takes a torch from the bucket drawer*)

Jacob. Where are you going?

Anna. Not far.

Jacob. Walking?

Anna. Yes, post a letter. (*She puts on her coat, scarf and gloves*)

(Mrs Hanker *hears Alvin and moves to the kitchen door, carrying the teacloth*)

Mrs Hanker. Alvin—where're you going?

Alvin. To hobby.

Mrs Hanker. You what?

Alvin. Hobby.

MRS HANKER. Hobby what?

ALVIN. Just hobby.

MRS HANKER (*going into the hall*) I said where're you going?

ALVIN (*picking up his wellingtons*) Walking.

MRS HANKER. And your tea? What about your tea?

ALVIN (*moving to the front door*) I'll have it for supper.

MRS HANKER (*following close behind Alvin*) You'll get it for breakfast if you don't.

ALVIN. All right.

MRS HANKER. Come back late.

(GEORGE *rises and peers round the kitchen door into the hall*)

ALVIN. All right. (*He leaves the front door and pauses outside to put his
ear to it*)

(MRS HANKER, *inside, puts her ear to the door.* ALVIN *goes to George's
bicycle and tries to remove the lamp*)

MRS HANKER (*calling*) You've got the keys?

(ALVIN *covers his mouth and shouts to simulate distance*)

ALVIN. Yeah.

(ALVIN *runs across the front of the stage and exits up* C. MRS HANKER
returns to the kitchen)

MRS HANKER. There—he's gone out.

GEORGE. Aye.

MRS HANKER. You can relax now.

GEORGE. Yes.

MRS HANKER. You don't need to feel you have to go to the club,
and you can dry for me. Here's the cloth.

(GEORGE *takes the teacloth and goes reluctantly to the sink*)

We'll clear these away, bank the fire up, sit down, switch the wire-
less, read the paper, hark at the wind and be glad we're warm inside
with—nothing but the hearthrug between us.

GEORGE. Nothing between us.

MRS HANKER. Snug, relaxed and comfortable.

GEORGE. Aye.

MRS HANKER. Lovely. (*She moves towards George*)

(GEORGE *tips his tea into the sink as the lights fade on the Hankers'
house* R. ANNA *picks up her letter and torch*)

JACOB. Come back soon.

ANNA. I will.

JACOB. I worry.

ANNA. You needn't.

JACOB. I do.

ANNA. You shouldn't.

ANNA *takes her beret from the hall-stand, puts it on, then goes out of the front door, and round the left side of the house to the forestage area down* L. *The lights fade on the Bowers' house* L *and come up on the down* L *and down* R *forestage areas.*

ALVIN *enters up* R *and comes down* R. *He pulls George's bicycle up stage of the curtain line and removes the cycle lamp.* ANNA *switches on the torch, looks at her letter, then shines the torch in her own face.* ALVIN *switches on the lamp and shines it in his face. They both look slowly up and out front as—*

the CURTAIN *falls*

ACT II

SCENE—*The same. Later the same evening.*

When the CURTAIN *rises the stage is in darkness, then the lights come up on the forestage area* LC. ALVIN *is on his hands and knees down* LC, *scraping earth out of the black box and putting it into his wellington boots. George's bicycle lamp is on the box in front of him. This is "Sledgewick's field". ANNA enters up* C *and comes silently down stage.* ALVIN's *back is towards her and when she reaches him she moves a little* L, *turns and shines her torch on to Alvin's face.*

ANNA. What are you doing?
ALVIN (*looking up; startled*) Digging.
ANNA. At night?
ALVIN. Yes.
ANNA. Without a spade?
ALVIN. Yes. I haven't got one.
ANNA. Aren't you trespassing?
ALVIN. I don't think so.
ANNA. You are. This is farmland. This field belongs to Mister Sledgewick.
ALVIN. I didn't know.
ANNA (*after a short pause*) Where do you live?
ALVIN. Calcutta Street.
ANNA. Where's that?
ALVIN. Off Bombay Road.
ANNA. Oh—Little India.
ALVIN. Yes.
ANNA. How long for?
ALVIN. Always.
ANNA. Then you must have known you were in Sledgewick field.
ALVIN. Yes, I know it's Sledgwick lane along here. (*He shines his torch on her face*)
ANNA. I live in Stroggen Hill Road.
ALVIN. That's the other one, isn't it?
ANNA. Along there, yes. At the junction.
ALVIN. I didn't know there was a man called Sledgewick.
ANNA. There is. (*She moves a little up* C) He owns this land.
ALVIN. I see.
ANNA (*after a pause*) He's a farmer. This soil is his. (*She pauses, turns and moves up* L *of Alvin*) You're stealing it, aren't you? (*She pauses*) Policemen come along here on their bicycles looking for couples. They shine their torches on the verge. Mister Sledgewick

won't have his private property used as a meeting place for young people to—to see each other in the dark. The police come. (*She crosses behind Alvin to* R *of him and points off* R *with her torch*) That's why it's deserted along here. There's "Do Not Trespass' signs farther down with fines written on them.

ALVIN. Oh.

ANNA. You can be prosecuted and fined for trespassing.

ALVIN. I see.

ANNA. And you *were* stealing, weren't you? (*She moves* RC *and looks off* R)

ALVIN. He won't miss a little bit of dirt.

ANNA (*turning and moving to* R *of Alvin*) If everybody took a little bit of Mister Sledgewick's field there'd soon be a hole.

ALVIN. If everybody took a bit, I wouldn't. I'd go somewhere else. I didn't know it was his field, anyway. I'd go in the public woods higher up and get some there.

ANNA. What do you want it for?

ALVIN (*after a pause*) It's my hobby.

ANNA. Collecting earth?

ALVIN. No. (*He pauses*) I grow plants in it.

ANNA. Oh. (*She pauses*) What kind?

ALVIN. Oh—flowers and things, you know, plants. Bulbs and flowering plants. (*He rises and collects his boots and torch*)

ANNA. I see. Your battery will run down. Hadn't you better turn it off?

ALVIN (*turning to face her*) 'S all right. (*He turns and moves up* C)

ANNA. If you're going into the wood to dig you'll need a strong light.

ALVIN (*stopping and turning*) I'll manage.

ANNA. Why don't you have a trowel to dig with? It's so much easier.

ALVIN (*moving down* C) I haven't got all the equipment I need— as yet. I will get one, though.

ANNA (*after a short pause*) Whose are those boots?

ALVIN. Mine.

ANNA. You'd better put them on if you're going into the woods.

ALVIN. I can't. I need them to put the dirt in.

ANNA. You should have a sack or a bag.

ALVIN. 'S all right.

ANNA. Why don't you buy soil from the shop?

ALVIN. It's not the same. It must be natural. A plant knows it's from the shop. It should be freshly dug up.

ANNA. I see.

ALVIN. Natural soil's best.

ANNA. Oh, I see. I grow daisies. Michaelmas daisies.

ALVIN. Ah, yes.

ANNA. What kind of plants are yours?

ALVIN. I don't remember their names. They're in Latin.

(*A torch suddenly flashes and wanders searchlight-wise round the fore-stage*)

ANNA. Ssssshshshs! (*She pushes Alvin down on the ground*) Down! (*She switches off her torch*)

(ALVIN *huddles himself above the box.* ANNA *goes up* C. *After a pause she comes down* C, *taps Alvin on the back with her torch, moves* RC *and looks off* R *to make sure all is clear.* ALVIN *kneels up and shines his torch on* ANNA'S *back and she turns to him*)

ALVIN. I'd better go to the woods and fill my boots.
ANNA. Yes.
ALVIN. I thought you were going to tell him.
ANNA. You go up Stroggen Hill Road. I'll walk you part way.

(ALVIN *rises*)

ANNA. Switch yours off, we'll use mine. (*She moves up* C)

(ALVIN *stamps the earth around the box to make it level.* ANNA *pauses, returns and helps* ALVIN.
        ALVIN *and* ANNA *look at each other, then exit up* C. *The lights fade* LC *and come up down* L.
        ANNA *and* ALVIN, *having walked around the back of the setting re-enter up* L *and come down* L *into the lights.* ANNA *arrives first, followed by* ALVIN)

What did you say your name was?
ALVIN. Alvin Hanker.
ANNA. Handcuff?
ALVIN. Hanker—H-A-N-K-E-R.
ANNA. You can take soil from my garden if you like.
ALVIN (*crossing below Anna to* R *of her*) I'd rather have it from the wood, thank you.
ANNA. I can lend you a shovel if you wait a minute.
ALVIN. I'll manage.
ANNA. Then take my torch. At least you'll be able to see what you're doing. (*She hands her torch to Alvin*) You can bring it back tomorrow. Or the next day. When you like.
ALVIN. Well, all right. I don't want to finish this battery. It's borrowed from a bicycle.
ANNA. It doesn't matter if the battery runs out in this. I keep a spare indoors.
ALVIN. Well—thank you. Good night. (*He crosses to* R)
ANNA (*calling after him*) There's plenty of leaf mould in the woods now. Better than Sledgewick's field. All clay there. And you won't need to hide from the policemen.
ALVIN. Good night.
ANNA. Good night.

(ALVIN *runs off up* R. ANNA *stares after him for a few moments then*

turns to go, stops, turns and looks after Alvin again. The lights BLACK-
OUT.

ANNA *exits down* L *in the* BLACK-OUT. *The lights come up on the
kitchen* R.

GEORGE *is sitting in the armchair. He is in his shirt-sleeves.*

MRS HANKER *is standing* R *of* GEORGE, *holding a tray with two
mugs of bedtime drink. The tin is also on the tray. She is in her dressing-
gown)*

MRS HANKER. This'll send you into sleep like the adverts. *(She
hands a mug to George)*

GEORGE. Thank you.

MRS HANKER. We'll drop off smiling and wake up gladly the day
after. *(She puts the tray on the table)*

GEORGE. You can't improve on a good night's rest. I like a good
night.

MRS HANKER *(picking up the tin and reading the label)* "Induces sleep,
deep and abiding." *(She replaces the tin and sits on the right arm of
George's chair. Suggestively)* There's other things do that besides hot
milk.

GEORGE *(looking pointedly at her)* Such as . . . ?

MRS HANKER. Other things.

GEORGE. Like what?

MRS HANKER. More than hot milk.

GEORGE. For instance?

MRS HANKER. A day's work.

GEORGE. That makes you tired.

MRS HANKER. And makes you sleep.

GEORGE. And what else "other things" besides?

MRS HANKER. Comforts. Warm comfort promotes rest in the
dark.

GEORGE. That's two other things.

MRS HANKER. That's work, hot milk and comfort.

GEORGE. You know what I'm thinking.

MRS HANKER. Don't ask me.

GEORGE. I'm telling you.

MRS HANKER. I know.

GEORGE. So . . .

MRS HANKER. I hear you.

GEORGE. So you know I've told you and I'm saying now we'll get
there in time, we'll come to that soon enough. There's plenty of
nights left for snoring in together. *(He rises, stretches and moves towards
the hall, still holding his mug)*

MRS HANKER. Where are you going?

GEORGE. I'm off up.

MRS HANKER. Why?

GEORGE. To get ready for the alarm. *(He goes upstairs into his room
and winds his alarm clock)*

The lights come up on George's room. The ticking of the alarm clock is heard through the loud-speakers throughout the scene)

MRS HANKER. It's coming on. I can feel it—it's nearer than that. The taste's approaching like blood in the mouth from a bit lip. There's time soon enough he says. I'll show him how to wait. I'll go after him. (*She rises and goes into the hall)* Out with the lights and follow him. Hot milk, work and comfort, there's three things to bring on the deep sleep and the law-abiding peace of a night-time.

(*The light fades on the kitchen.* GEORGE, *after winding his clock, removes his shirt and trousers and puts them over the chair at the foot of the bed. He then puts on his pyjama trousers)*

(*She whispers)* I'm getting to feel the pain of being on a different floor. I can't bear the ceiling between us. Don't let him leave you down here. Go on, up, go to bed, drink your milk, sleep if you can, rest in the dark. (*She goes slowly upstairs and pauses on the landing)* I'll have to put up with the walls for a time—so long as we're on the same floor. I must be on his level. (*She starts towards her bedroom but returns to lean an ear against George's door)*

(GEORGE, *on the inside, does the same thing. He and* MRS HANKER *both listen)*

You know what he's thinking. (*She goes into her bedroom, puts her mug on her bedside table, switches on the lamp, turns back the bed-cover, takes off her dressing gown and lays it on the bed, and then gets into bed)*

(*The lights come up on Mrs Hanker's room.* GEORGE *puts on his pyjama jacket and gets into bed)*

The nights are drawing in and so's George. Things are nearly closer. In a short while he'll put the light out for me. (*She switches out her light)*

(*Simultaneously, the lights fade on Mrs Hanker's and George's rooms)*

Beside. Next to. Don't palpitate. Good night, Ivy. (*She pauses)* Don't sleep, George. Don't leave me here—awake.

(ALVIN *enters up* R, *goes down* R *and replaces the lamp on George's bicycle. He comes into the house, wipes his feet and drops his wellingtons. He makes a noise removing his coat and putting it on the hall-stand. This wakes* GEORGE *and* MRS HANKER, *who sit up in bed)*

He's coming now.
GEORGE. I didn't lock the door.
MRS HANKER. He's creeping for me in the dark.
GEORGE. If she's coming to crawl between the bedclothes without the light on, I can't prevent her.
MRS HANKER. I'll pretend to sleep.

GEORGE. She's in for a big surprise when she gets here. Bigger than she expects. I can't prevent it.

(ALVIN *picks up his wellingtons and goes upstairs, lighting his way with Anna's torch*)

MRS HANKER. Come on, George.
GEORGE. Here you are, Ivy.

(ALVIN *goes into his room, slamming the door behind him.* MRS HANKER *and* GEORGE *are startled*)

MRS HANKER. If he thinks I'm going to lie here while he decides to go back to his bed he's mistaken. (*She switches on her lamp and gets out of bed*)

(*The lights come up on Mrs Hanker's room*)

GEORGE. I don't think I locked the door. I'd better check. (*He gets out of bed*)

(*The lights come up on George's room.* MRS HANKER *and* GEORGE *each go to their doors, pause a second to listen then step out on to the landing and meet just outside George's door*)

MRS HANKER. I thought you'd be over there.
GEORGE. I thought I'd locked the door.
MRS HANKER. I thought I heard you moving.
GEORGE. I thought you were.
MRS HANKER. Happen it was Alvin coming in. (*She calls*) Alvin.

(*She moves to Alvin's door, opens it and puts her head inside*)

(ALVIN *hides, crouching behind the door*)

Alvin, did you come in?

(ALVIN *is silent*)

No, he's not back. (*She closes the door and turns to George*)
GEORGE. It must have been you I heard.
MRS HANKER. Or else I heard you more like.

(*There is a long pause. They look at each other*)

It's cold out here.

(GEORGE *takes off his pyjama jacket and puts it minkwise round her shoulders*)

There's not much warmth in a 'jama jacket.
GEORGE. Well, you're not getting the trousers.
MRS HANKER. I never asked for the jacket.
GEORGE (*after a short pause*) Good night, then. (*He moves towards his bedroom*)
MRS HANKER (*intercepting George*) My husband had a dressing-gown made of white towels that our Alvin gave him as a present.

C

Lovely white towels that would have wrapped you up warm. You could have put it on if Alvin hadn't taken it as his own. (*Still looking at George she moves to Alvin's door*)

(GEORGE *follows Mrs Hanker*)

In fact if you'll stay there shivering I'll get it and you shall have it to wear for the future. (*She opens Alvin's door and goes inside*)

(GEORGE *stands at the door.* MRS HANKER *trips over one of Alvin's boots, then with* GEORGE *watching she reaches behind the door for a white dressing-gown which is hanging there. It falls on* ALVIN *who shines the torch on to Mrs Hanker's face. He is kneeling.* MRS HANKER *falls back against the chest of drawers, screaming*)

Aaaaaaarrhkk! Alvin! What are you doing crouched up in the dark for?

ALVIN. Get out.

MRS HANKER. What's all this——

ALVIN. Leave it.

MRS HANKER. —this dirt in your boots?

ALVIN. Take what you've come for and get back where you came from.

MRS HANKER. Where did you get that torch?

ALVIN. Stay out of me. Get away.

MRS HANKER. Why didn't you answer when I called?

ALVIN. Never say a word to me unless you're asked. It's my turn for that.

MRS HANKER (*concerned*) Alvin . . .

ALVIN. Don't call me that.

MRS HANKER. What's the matter, love?

ALVIN. Nor that. (*He throws the dressing-gown at her*) Here—take the dead man's towelling and get out. (*He rises*)

MRS HANKER. Hoh!

ALVIN (*pushing her out of the room*) Drape it on Mister Bland and don't come back.

MRS HANKER. Alvin . . . (*She falls against George*)

ALVIN (*standing squarely on the threshold of his bedroom door*) If you touch this door knob again I'll unhinge it and bash your head in.

MRS HANKER (*whispering*) George . . . (*She moves behind George*)

ALVIN. You're wanted, Mister Bland. You're a man wanted without a reward.

MRS HANKER. George, don't let him.

(GEORGE *moves slightly towards Alvin*)

ALVIN (*shining the torch in George's face*) Never talk to me.

MRS HANKER. There's something wrong with him.

ALVIN. Never breathe in my room.

MRS HANKER. He's breaking down in pieces in front of us.

ALVIN. It's my room.

Mrs Hanker. He needs to see the proper people to tell him what to do.

Alvin. I live in my room. I'm entitled. I have permission.

Mrs Hanker. He can't go on like this. Mrs Raistrick'll hear him and be able to tell what he's saying.

(George *backs away.* Mrs Hanker *moves forward*)

Alvin. I put the paper to the walls, I nailed the linoleum, the rugs are where I left them and I played the gramophone—I deserve these things.

Mrs Hanker. You need a change.

Alvin. I belong to my room.

Mrs Hanker. Why don't you go abroad?

Alvin. I'm the one for my room, you're for yours and don't forget it.

Mrs Hanker. Why don't you go mad and have done?

Alvin. I'll do nothing for your peace of mind. Turn away. Please. Please turn the other way so I can close the door.

(Mrs Hanker *turns away, crying. She cuddles her face in the dressing-gown.* George *turns to her and rests a hand on her pyjama jacketed shoulder.* Alvin *closes the door, hiding behind it.* George *and* Mrs Hanker *look at the door then at each other.* Mrs Hanker *lowers her eyes and looks across* George's *rising chest*)

Mrs Hanker. A chestful of skin like semolina pudding with a ripe currant on either side as punctuation. (*She puts the dressing-gown over George's shoulders, crombie-wise*) This is the one. Lovely white towels that wrap you up warm.

George (*after a pause*) Close your door, then. (*He goes into his room*)

(Mrs Hanker *pulls the pyjama jacket farther on to her shoulders, goes into her room and switches off the light. The lights fade on* Mrs Hanker's *room.* Mrs Hanker *crosses the landing and goes into George's room.* George *takes off the dressing-gown and* Mrs Hanker *removes the pyjama jacket. The lights fade to* Black-Out.

George *and* Mrs Hanker *exit in the* Black-Out. *The lights come up on Alvin's room.* Alvin *is sitting in the chair, reading the gardening book*)

Alvin (*reading as he turns the pages*) "The dog-tail *Borealis— Obscurus—Floribisca—Ad Lybia Prim-ul-aris—Uvula-Laryh-gina—Som-nambular-Omni-bus-cum — Orchis-Pa-eonie-Glutunus-Max-omus — Daf-o-dil . . .*" Daffodil. "*Ovular-ovum-Flori-bis-cus—Nomine-Sanc-tum-sar-cofungus—Lili-orum Volvus—Liliorum Volvus——*

(*The slow scholarly voice of the* Author *of the book is heard over the speaker's*)

Author. —commonly known as Dragon's fang."

ALVIN. Dragon's fang.

AUTHOR. "This lily is a prime favourite with all true British flower lovers. It is thought to have been introduced to these shores by Alvin Alleynburgh, a minstrel and a player of the flute who served King Richard the Lionheart during that gallant monarch's crusades to the Holy Land."

ALVIN. Alvin Alleynburgh.

AUTHOR. "*Liliorum Volvus* Culture. The Volvus Lily is best suited to a fibrous loamy soil. Textbooks tell us that Dragon's Fang likes leaf-mould and a little bit of decayed compost, and while I have no wish to dispute the verity of their recommendation nor argue with their authority I must record my experience that half a bushel of road scrapings, well watered, does this lily a power of good. Take any box . . ."

ALVIN. Take any box. (*He puts the open book on the stool, rises, moves the chair down stage out of the way, then takes a box and a milk bottle with some water from under the chest of drawers. He kneels and arranges the articles and his wellingtons around him. He kneels so that the book on the stool is in front of him. He finds the place in the book and reads*) "Take any box."

AUTHOR. "Take any box and fill with the mixture."

(ALVIN *tips the earth from the wellingtons into the empty box and pats it level then reads the book again*)

"Make an oval in the centre, six inches deep—and twice the width of your bulb. Sprinkle the bottom with fine silver sand."

(ALVIN *sprinkles sand from a cloth bag then reads the book again*)

"Add water till moist——"

(ALVIN *pours water from a milk bottle then consults the book*)

"—and stir."

(ALVIN *stirs with his finger*)

"Place the bulb in the centre."

(ALVIN *hurriedly scrapes the wet earth from his stirring finger on to the sides of the box, then picks up the bulb. He holds it delicately between finger and thumb and rotates his wrist, admiring the bulb*)

(*Slightly irritated*) "Place the bulb in the centre——"

(ALVIN *kisses the bulb, places it in the box and tips the rest of the soil from the wellingtons on to it. The inner sole from the boot falls out and he throws it away*)

"—and lightly pack with dry, turfy loam."

(ALVIN *covers the box with the lid*)

"*Liliorum Volvus* will not endure draughts in the early stages of its growth, so cover it in a warm and sheltered spot, out of harm's way."

ALVIN (*looking at the door of his room*) Out of harm's way . . . (*He rises, takes the box to the wardrobe, puts it inside and closes the door, then goes to the chair, sits and picks up the book*)

AUTHOR. "Water every seven days——"

ALVIN. Every seven days.

AUTHOR. "—for several weeks."

ALVIN. For several weeks.

AUTHOR. "At the end of two months remove and report."

ALVIN. Remove and report. (*He closes the book, puts it on the chest of drawers beside him, rises, goes to the wardrobe and opens the door*)

(*The lights* BLACK-OUT *for a few moments to indicate the passing of two months.* ALVIN *takes out of the wardrobe a pot with a small shoot which he holds up for a moment then lovingly places on the stool. The lights come up on the kitchen. Music, "La Mer" is coming from the radio.*

MRS HANKER *enters up* C *through the back door, comes into the kitchen, picks up the garbage bucket and goes into the hall*)

MRS HANKER (*calling*) Alvin! (*She goes out and empties the garbage into the dustbin*)

ALVIN (*to his plant*) See you tonight. (*He goes downstairs, leaves his overall in the hall and sits at the kitchen table*)

(MRS HANKER *picks up a pint of milk from outside the front door and goes into the hall*)

MRS HANKER (*calling*) Alvin! (*She goes into the kitchen and is annoyed to see Alvin already in place. She places the garbage bucket above the stove, then pours milk on to Alvin's cereal*) Well. How long is this going on? (*She washes up some dishes*)

(*There is silence.* ALVIN *ignores her. He is now quite tidy with a collar and tie. He looks calm and serene*)

When do you intend to stop it? (*She pauses*) You needn't think you worry us not talking day in and out. We've got other things to do than get concerned about whether or not we should listen to your silences and not-speaking-to-us attitude. (*She pauses*) How do you get on at work? (*She pauses*) I expect you've plenty to say for yourself there, unless you've gone to Coventry (*She pauses*)

(ALVIN *holds out his empty bowl*)

(*She snatches the bowl from Alvin and washes it up*) When you think you'd like to use your tongue again and say a few words I hope you don't expect we'll listen to you. (*She pauses*)

(ALVIN *eats bread and butter*)

We shan't. (*She pauses*) You'll talk to yourself. (*She pauses*)

(ALVIN *rises and goes into the hall, where he takes his scarf from the hall-stand and puts it on*)

(*She does not realize that she is alone*) Anyone who's not bothered to talk to his mother or the postman for as many weeks as you have, can't presume there'll be ears ready to listen to owt he has to say if and when he should want to sometime in the future.

(ALVIN *looks into the imaginary mirror and tidies his hair*)

So don't presume it in this house. (*She turns, realizes Alvin has gone and follows him into the hall*) It's been a blessing to have you shut up. You can't think how glad we are that you've gone into yourself and left me alone, peaceful.

(ALVIN *sits on the stairs and puts on his shoes*)

Mrs Raistrick's not had anything to knock on the door or bang the back gate for four weeks or more. She's the only one who's missed your noises that you used to make. (*She pauses*)

(ALVIN *rises, walks around Mrs Hanker to the hall-stand and takes down his jacket*)

You must think we don't like it to hear you not saying anything. (*She pauses*)

(ALVIN *puts his jacket on*)

Well, you're wrong. It matters nothing to us. We have our own lives to live without unspoken interferences from you so you needn't think it.

ANNOUNCER (*through the radio*) The time is five minutes to eight.

MRS HANKER (*going into the kitchen; furiously*) The time is five minutes to eight.

ANNOUNCER (*through the radio*) Here is the weather forecast . . .

(MRS HANKER *switches off the radio, then goes to the stove, picks up Alvin's thermos flask and tucks it under her arm*)

MRS HANKER. If you go now you'll be in time for the bus.

(ALVIN *comes into the kitchen, picks up his sandwich box, sees his thermos and takes it from Mrs Hanker. He tries to exit by the back door but* MRS HANKER *bars his way. He turns and goes into the hall*)

(*She follows Alvin*) I suppose you know what you're doing, putting your coat on and leaving in time so's you're not late, because *I* don't. (*She pauses*)

(ALVIN *collects his overalls, goes out of the front door, crosses to* C, *then moves up* C *and exits*)

(*She follows Alvin*) I don't care if you're on time to work or too early for the one after or if you get a seat. (*She moves* C) You don't vex me with your silent punctuality so you can grow out of it as soon as you like. Insolence. (*She follows Alvin up* C) What have you got upstairs? What are you doing? (*She returns to the kitchen through the back door and goes to the sink*) Scarcely three minutes before eight and he's left me with the washing-up. He needn't think I'm won by not opening his mouth in front of me. Who does he think he is? The pigging bleeder. I'll ruddy well find out what he's up to upstairs. I'll find out and stop it. Put a good stop to it. That'll make him talk. The donkey-nosed, stuck-up muling fat ass. Nobody doesn't talk to me without saying a word. He wasn't born dumb like some poor kids. (*She moves to the table*) God let him have a tongue and I'll have it out —as his mother I'll see he uses it. (*She picks up a plate from the table and crashes it down against the metal corner, breaking it like a gramophone record, into many pieces*) Hhoooohuohhoo! (*She weeps*) That's right, break my dinner plates. You see what you've done? I'll tell George. (*She goes on to her hands and knees and tries to pick up the pieces*) He's broken it, he'll pay for it, I shan't. He'll have to pay for it. I'll cry till George brings the post. I'll have to get rid of it somehow—or nobody'll care a damn. (*She leans on the right arm of the armchair and sobs*)

(*The lights fade on the kitchen.* MRS HANKER *removes her apron in the* BLACK-OUT.

GEORGE *enters in the* BLACK-OUT *and sits in the armchair in the kitchen, reading a newspaper.*

ALVIN, *also in the* BLACK-OUT, *enters his room through the false wardrobe back and changes the plant on the stool for a larger one. When the lights come up* ALVIN *is sitting, reading the gardening book.* MRS HANKER *is standing in the hall, listening to Alvin as he reads*)

ALVIN (*reading*) "At this stage in the growth of the *Liliorum Volvus* the leaves should be uniformly elongated in outline and pale green in colour." (*He picks up the plant and looks at it then replaces it on the stool*) "If any irregularities occur prior to bud growth, snip or twitch off every alternate leaf starting at the base of the stem." You grow all right as you are without a book of rules. (*He slams the book shut and puts it on the chest of drawers*) It's an old-fashioned book of rules, anyway. I'll get a new one. (*He rises and strokes the leaves of the plant*) You'll be the best ever grown when you've finished. (*He whispers*) Biggest—sharpest—widest—tallest—bestest.

MRS HANKER (*going into the kitchen*) He talks to himself all right, all day.

GEORGE. He *never* spoke to me so I don't miss it.

MRS HANKER (*kneeling* R *of George*) Won't you, can't you ask him, darling? Find out what it is he's got and let's get to the bottom of it.

(ALVIN *puts on his jacket and leaves his room, leaving the plant on the stool. He locks the door behind him*)

GEORGE. We never had two words to rub together, Alvin and me. I doubt if anything I might say to him on your behalf would bring us into conversational terms now. It's something we went without. However . . .

MRS HANKER. I knew you would. (*She rises*)

(ALVIN *goes quickly down the stairs, out of the front door and exits down* R)

GEORGE. Too late. He's gone out.

MRS HANKER (*moving* R) You're always in time for getting out of things these days. It spells unwillingness to me.

(*There is a pause*)

GEORGE Come here.

(MRS HANKER *moves reluctantly to George*)

MRS HANKER. I have done. What now?

GEORGE. You see this thigh?

MRS HANKER. I do.

GEORGE. Well, sit on it.

(MRS HANKER *sits on George's lap*)

You'll find out soon enough when I'm unwilling. I'm the one to register any lack of readiness not you. So sit quiet.

MRS HANKER. If and as how you're ready and willing still, why don't you do me a favour?

GEORGE. Like . . . ?

MRS HANKER. Borrowing Raistrick's ladder next door and having a go at some upstair-window cleaning. With a leather and a ladling can, you could do them in ten minutes' time and they'd sparkle for the week-end. Don't forget when this afternoon's over, it'll be Saturday night.

GEORGE. You mean you'd withhold inclination?

MRS HANKER. I mean one good turn deserves the other.

GEORGE. You'll get your good turn whether or not I rub down the windows, I'll see to that. You think the day matters?

MRS HANKER. I do, it does and it will. Friday's bath night.

GEORGE. Well?

MRS HANKER. Saturday's psychological. (*She rises and moves* R)

(GEORGE *gives in, rises, and goes to the kitchen door*)

GEORGE. Fill the ladling can and get the leather out till I get the ladder.

(GEORGE *exits up* R. MRS HANKER *smiles and goes to the sink, gets the ladling can, fills it with water and exits through the back door, up* C. *The lights fade on the kitchen and come up on the forestage.*

ANNA *enters down* R *and crosses to* C. *She is in the library. She looks out front as if surveying the bookshelves. She carries a book, a handbag and library tickets. She stands on the box down* LC.

ALVIN *enters simultaneously down* L, *also looking at the shelves. He notices Anna on the box, crosses above to* R *of her, then moves towards her to speak.* ANNA *speaks mainly out front, turning occasionally to him*)

ALVIN. Hello.

ANNA. Hello.

ALVIN. I've still got your torch.

ANNA. Shshshsh! You're not supposed to talk in libraries.

ALVIN. You can whisper.

ANNA (*after a pause*) I don't need it.

ALVIN. What?

ANNA. My torch.

ALVIN. You said you had another one.

ANNA (*after a short pause*) You got the earth you wanted?

ALVIN. Leaf-mould, yes.

ANNA. Good.

ALVIN. And I planted a bulb.

ANNA (*turning to him*) Did it grow?

ALVIN. Yes, very much, thank you. It's called "*Liliorum Volvus*".

ANNA. Dragon's Fang.

ALVIN. How did you know?

ANNA. My father has a book. I read it once.

ALVIN. I've seen you in here before.

ANNA. I wondered where we had.

ALVIN. Met before?

ANNA. Where we'd met before, yes.

ALVIN. Before we met in the field?

ANNA. Yes, before last time. When we met last time I thought I'd seen you before somewhere else.

ALVIN. It was in here. Lending books.

ANNA. Borrowing.

ALVIN. What are you taking out?

ANNA. I haven't decided.

ALVIN. Those are Geographical.

ANNA. My brother's a seaman. I chart his voyages on maps.

ALVIN. I want *Bot*anical.

ANNA. Bot*anical*. (*She points* R) Over there.

(ALVIN *moves* R *then turns back*)

ALVIN. If you come with me to my house you can have your torch back. (*He pauses*) It's not far.

ANNA. All right. (*She steps backwards from the box*)

ALVIN. I'll wait for you at the "Way Out".

ANNA. I'm going now.

ALVIN. Oh.

ANNA. Shall I wait there for you?

ALVIN. All right. (*He goes quickly down* R, *looking at the shelves*)

ANNA (*following Alvin*) If you come with me to Byeways you could borrow my father's *Gardening Encyclopaedia*. (*She pauses*) You won't need to renew it.

ALVIN. All right.

(ANNA *turns, crosses and exits down* L.

ALVIN *crosses and follows her off. The lights fade on the forestage and come up on the kitchen* R.

GEORGE *enters quickly up* R, *holding a ladder and smoking a cigarette. He comes down* R, *crosses to* C, *then goes up* C.

MRS HANKER *enters up* C, *holding the can and wash leather*)

MRS HANKER. That's right. Careful. Hold it up. There you go. My word. Here's your can. (*She gives him the wash leather and can*)

(GEORGE *and* MRS HANKER *vanish behind the set and are heard but not seen till* GEORGE *has set up the ladder outside Alvin's window, climbs it and is peering in the window*)

Well, what do you see?

GEORGE. Nothing to mention.

MRS HANKER. Open up and climb in. Exploring's the only way to discovery.

(GEORGE *pushes the window up, puts one leg over the sill and sits astride it, facing* L. MRS HANKER's *face appears up the ladder.* GEORGE *reaches in and puts the can and leather on the chest of drawers.* MRS HANKER *is now visible from the waist upwards*)

You ought to have been a window-cleaner, it suits you from below.

GEORGE. What does?

MRS HANKER. Sitting astride it like that, one in, one out.

GEORGE. One what?

MRS HANKER. You know what.

GEORGE. Say it, then.

MRS HANKER. You always pester me to mouth it.

GEORGE. Because you hold back.

MRS HANKER. Because I'm not forward.

GEORGE. You've reformed then.

MRS HANKER. Who said it was a drawback being forward. Holding back's nothing to reform to nor be proud of.

GEORGE. Say it, then.

MRS HANKER. What?

GEORGE. Sitting astride, you said.

MRS HANKER. Window-sill, I meant.

GEORGE. One in, one out, you said.

MRS HANKER. You like to hear the sound of your own body, that's your trouble.

GEORGE. One what?

MRS HANKER. Thigh.

GEORGE. Where?

MRS HANKER. In. One thigh in.

GEORGE. And out?

MRS HANKER. The other. One thigh in the other out. Are you atisfied? I always have to clarify. You'd kill anyone's spontaneity you would. You strangle me dry. I have enough of your thighs at night without having them forced down my throat in broad daylight.

GEORGE. You brought them up.

MRS HANKER. I never mentioned them. (*She looks at George's thigh*)

GEORGE. You hinted.

MRS HANKER. Not by name, though.

GEORGE. A hint's a good as done.

MRS HANKER. No. Spontaneous hinting's allowed. It's different to naming. (*She runs her palm along the top of his thigh*) I said sitting astride suits you. It does. Just look at that. Did you ever see such a thigh on a window-sill? Curving up to the knee before dangling over the edge. It's worth climbing anybody's ladder to look at. (*She peers into the room and notices the plant*) What's that?

GEORGE. What?

MRS HANKER (*pointing*) That. That's it. That's what he's got that he won't let me discover. That's what he won't tell me. Get in.

(ALVIN *and* ANNA *enter up* R *and go down* R, *pause for a moment to look at George's bike, then enter the hall.* GEORGE *has trouble swinging his leg into the room and sprawls into the room, knocking the plant off the stool. The noise makes* ALVIN *rush upstairs and unlock the door.* ANNA *remains in the hall*)

You're not clumsy, are you? Blind hunchbacks aren't a patch on you.

(GEORGE, *still on his knees, picks up the plant and puts it on the stool.* ALVIN *stands in the doorway*)

GEORGE (*still on his knees; apologetically*) I was cleaning your windows. It got knocked by accident. I am sorry. It's all right. No damage. No damage done. It's very nice. We were admiring it. Your mother and me. (*He rises*) We were saying how tall it was for a plant that size. What sort is it? With soot off the windows you should get more sunlight through—do it good.

MRS HANKER. George.

GEORGE. Ivy?

MRS HANKER. Why do you let him listen to you without replying?

GEORGE. He makes me feel guilty.

MRS HANKER. He thinks he's getting at me through you. Pass me that plant. I'll make him talk with it.

(GEORGE *hesitates*)

Go on—reach over and give it to me here. We'll see what it's like from the first floor. Dropped out from the ladder top. When it's down on the flags in the back he'll find his God-given tongue. He'll call out and use it like he used to then. If you want to hear his voice, pass it over, George. We'll make him live with us.

(GEORGE *hesitates*)

I'm waiting.

(GEORGE *does not move*)

If you don't do it, George, if you don't do as I ask you're a postman.
Not worth a lick on a stamp.

(GEORGE *picks up the plant.* ALVIN *stares incredulously.* MRS HANKER
holds out her hands to receive the plant. ALVIN *looks from George to the
plant then at Mrs Hanker. He shakes his head from side to side and is
about to say something, but controls himself, shutting his mouth. He picks
up the ladling can from the chest and throws the water from it into Mrs
Hanker's face.* MRS HANKER *screws up her eyes tight as the water hits
her in the face. She clasps her outstretched hands over her mouth as she
screams. She falls backwards away from the ladder and down on to the
paving stones in the yard below.* ALVIN *throws the empty ladling can out of
the window. It clatters as it lands in the yard*)

GEORGE (*rushing to the window*) Oh, my God, what's happened?

(ANNA *goes half-way up the stairs.*
GEORGE *turns to Alvin, thrusts the plant into his hands, then climbs
out of the window and down the ladder.* ALVIN *slams the window shut,
picks up Anna's torch and still clutching the plant, goes downstairs*)

ALVIN (*handing the torch to Anna*) Here it is. (*He passes Anna and
goes into the hall*)

ANNA. Thank you.

ALVIN. This is my plant.

ANNA. It's very strong.

ALVIN. Yes, but it needs the sunlight.

ANNA. I thought I heard a scream.

ALVIN. My mother fell off a ladder, round the back.

ANNA. Had she a weak heart?

ALVIN. No.

ANNA. My mother fell down a flight of stairs and died at the
bottom, but she had a weak heart.

ALVIN (*indicating the plant*) She was throwing it away. It's not safe
to leave. It's getting too big and needs the sunlight. I'll turn it loose.
I'll plant it in the woods.

ANNA. There's a greenhouse in our garden. You can use it if you
like.

ALVIN. To live in, you mean?

ANNA. No. For your plant.

ALVIN (*stepping up to her; vehemently*) It's not only that. I'm getting
past living here, as well. It's not safe for either of us.

ANNA (*alarmed*) Oh. (*She comes downstairs into the hall*)

ALVIN. I'm sorry your mother had a weak heart when she died.

ANNA. That's all right. She was old.

(GEORGE *rushes in up* c *and comes through the kitchen into the hall*)

GEORGE (*agitatedly*) Alvin . . . (*He sees Anna*) Oh—hello. It's Miss Bowers, isn't it?

(ALVIN *moves into the kitchen*)

ANNA. Yes.

GEORGE. I can always place the name when I see the face. Excuse me. (*He turns to Alvin*) Alvin, she's knocked out or something, concussed and bleeding, too, a bit. You'll have to fetch the doctor.

ALVIN. I haven't got a bicycle. You'd get there first on the bike.

GEORGE. Well, all right, but you get her inside.

ANNA. You shouldn't move her unless she's dead.

ALVIN. I can't stop now, anyway. I'm going to Stroggen Hill Road before it's too dark. (*He goes into the hall*)

GEORGE. Alvin . . .

ALVIN (*ignoring George; to Anna*) Miss Bowers——

ANNA. Yes, Mister Hanker?

ALVIN. —could I let a room in your house, do you think?

ANNA. Yes, I think I could arrange it.

ALVIN. Tonight?

ANNA. Yes.

ALVIN. Thank you. (*He goes out of the front door*)

GEORGE. You ought to stay, Alvin. She's your mother.

ALVIN (*turning to George*) Ask Mrs Raistrick. It's her ladder she climbed.

ANNA. Good afternoon. (*She goes out of the front door*)

(ALVIN *crosses to* c. *He stops and turns for a moment as* ANNA *hesitates*)

GEORGE (*going out of the front door and calling*) Now, Alvin . . .

(ALVIN *turns and exits up* c.
ANNA *follows Alvin off.*
GEORGE *rushes to his bicycle, mounts it and rides off up* R. *The lights fade on the house* R *and come up on the living-room* L.
ANNA *and* ALVIN *enter up* L *and go into the living-room.* ANNA *moves to the sewing-table, puts her torch in the drawer, then puts her bag on the chair. She motions to Alvin to put the plant on the table*)

ANNA. Shall I take your coat?

ALVIN *puts the plant on the sewing-table, unfastens his donkey jacket, turns his back to* ANNA *who helps him off with the coat.* ALVIN *sees the nude dummy and does a "double-take", then turns to his plant as—*

the CURTAIN *falls*

ACT III

SCENE—*The same. A day or two later. Evening.*

In the Bowers' living-room the furniture has been moved. The magazin rack has gone. The sewing-table is L *with an additional upright chair ane the wheel-chair above it. The wheel-chair is* L. *The original chair is now* R *Alvin's room is bare and tidy, with the stool on top of the chest of drawers. The record player has gone.*

When the CURTAIN *rises, the stage is in darkness, then the lights come up on the Bowers' house* L. JACOB *is seated in his wheel-chair.* ALVIN *is seated* R *of Jacob. They are playing snakes and ladders.* ANNA *is seated* R *knitting baby clothes.*

ALVIN. You to fifty-eight. I'm on forty-two.

JACOB (*shaking the dice*) I haven't played snakes and ladders since I was a child.

ANNA. Yes, you have. (*To Alvin*) He has. Many a time. With Maurice and Clifford when they were boys. (*To Jacob*) You used to have contests. The three of you.

(JACOB *throws the dice*)

JACOB. Six and two.

ALVIN. Eight. To sixty-six.

JACOB (*moving his counter*) Missed it.

(ALVIN *and* JACOB *"freeze" as Anna speaks*)

ANNA (*to herself*) They used to have contests, between them, the three of them. I wasn't allowed as a girl because I was young, too young and a girl.

(ALVIN *and* JACOB *resume playing.* ALVIN *shakes the dice and throws them*)

ALVIN. Three one.

JACOB. Three and one.

ALVIN (*moving his counter*) Four—to forty-two, forty-six. Down.

JACOB. You've hit a snake. You're eaten, beaten. Down to fourteen. Bad luck. Never mind. My turn. (*He collects the dice*)

(ALVIN *and* JACOB *"freeze" as Anna speaks*)

ANNA (*to herself*) When I *was* old enough to join them they'd grown out of it, my brother and he, so I played by myself for two players. Alone but as two, with one red one green. For the red counter I shook them with my left hand and for the green I used the right. Red nearly always won, which was strange. I'm not left-handed.

(ALVIN *and* JACOB *resume playing.* JACOB *throws the dice*)

JACOB. Three and three. Six. And a double shake for a pair. Six to sixty-six. (*He moves his counter*)
ALVIN. Seventy-two.
ANNA. Sounds like father's ahead.

(JACOB *shakes the dice*)

ALVIN. Yes. He is.
ANNA (*to Alvin*) Shake with the left hand, that's how to win.

(JACOB *throws the dice*)

JACOB. And nine is eighty-one. (*He moves his counter*) Two rungs up to ninety-four. Your turn.

(ALVIN *collects the dice and shakes them*)

ANNA (*to Alvin*) How did you play your games without any brothers and sisters?
ALVIN. My dad would play. He liked a game indoors. (*He throws the dice*) To twenty-five and up to fifty-seven. (*He moves his counter*) Ludo, draughts, tiddly-winks and a Lexicon pack.

(JACOB *collects the dice and shakes them frantically*)

(*To Jacob*) You need six to win, no more. (*To Anna*) Dad bought them for both of us. The bagatelle was his birthday surprise.

(JACOB *and* ALVIN *"freeze" as Anna speaks*)

ANNA. Father gets too excited. He forgets it's only a game. He forgets the time and what the doctor tells him. (*She picks up her knitting bag and pattern on her chair*) Come along. Put it away. (*She goes between Jacob and Alvin, collects the counters and dice and puts them in the shaker, then picks up the board and folds it*) It's only a game and father has won. (*She picks up the box and puts the board, etc., into it*)

(JACOB *and* ALVIN *relax*)

JACOB. I don't want to go.

(ALVIN *rises angrily and moves* R)

ANNA. Come along. (*To Alvin*) There's nothing more to bring from Calcutta Street?
ALVIN. I cleared everything out.
ANNA. I'll make a space in the stair cupboard. We'll keep them in there. Except the record-player, of course. (*She puts the box on the table*)
JACOB. How's your baby knitting for the Elephant stall?

ANNA (*pulling the wheel-chair up* R) I'll worry about that when you're tucked in bed. Say good night.

(ANNA *helps* JACOB *from the wheel-chair and upstairs to his room*)

JACOB. Good night.
ALVIN. Good night.
JACOB. Good night. I haven't played since I was a boy.
ANNA. You played with Maurice and Clifford many a time. You had contests.

(JACOB *removes his dressing-gown and gets into bed.* ANNA *closes the window curtains, lays the dressing-gown on the foot of the bed, bends over and kisses Jacob's forehead.*

ALVIN *takes the torch from the sewing-table and exits up* L.

ANNA *pauses on the stairs, registers Alvin's absence, looks in the table drawer, then collects her cardigan from the back of her chair, puts it over her shoulders and exits up* L. *The lights fade on the Bowers' house* L *and come up on the forestage area down* C.

ALVIN *enters up* C *and comes down* C. *He carries a small step-ladder, with a thermometer attached to the left side of it. The lily, now big and strong, is on the top of the ladder with the torch.* ALVIN *carries the ladder down* C *and places it* R *of the box down* LC. *We are in the greenhouse.* ALVIN *studies the plant and talks to it.*

ALVIN. You're the tallest that ever grew. (*He fondles the leaves up the step until he reaches the bud. He caresses the bud with a finger-tip then brushes his lips against it. He cradles it in his palms and breathes in as though syphoning the flower's future fragrance from the stem, as though coaxing the bloom from the bud*)

(ANNA *enters up* C *and comes down* C. *She carries a small coal shovel and glove*)

ANNA (*moving to* L *of Alvin*) I couldn't find the torch.
ALVIN. I borrowed it.
ANNA. I see. I came for a few pieces of coal. (*She puts the shovel on the ground beside the ladder*)
ALVIN. I'll bring some. (*He circles the plant on the ladder and trips over the shovel*)
ANNA. Thank you. (*She moves up* C *and pauses briefly*)
ALVIN. Close the door. The heat escapes.
ANNA (*turning and moving to* L *of Alvin*) It doesn't stick any more.
ALVIN. Winter made the wood swell. It was damp.
ANNA. The heat's dried it.
ALVIN. That's right.
ANNA. What's the temperature?
ALVIN (*looking at the thermometer*) Sixty-eight. (*He moves* L *of the plant*)
ANNA (*moving to* R *of the plant and looking at it*) It's very strong.
ALVIN. Yes.

ANNA. So tall.

ALVIN. It's going to flower soon. You can see the petals.

ANNA. If it weren't going to flower before July you could have put it in the Show.

ALVIN. I thought about it.

ANNA. It will flower, though.

ALVIN. I know, and die before then.

ANNA. You encouraged it too much too soon for July.

ALVIN. If it hadn't been going to flower then and if I'd put it in would it have won first place, do you think?

ANNA. I don't suppose so. But it would have been nice for it to be there with the others. (*She touches the plant*)

ALVIN. I wouldn't have liked it to be second best or third or without a place altogether.

ANNA. Nothing is.

ALVIN. After the way it's grown it deserves to be more.

ANNA. Nothing can. If it's grown it has and that's it. You don't compete, you can't. You grow and put in for the display.

ALVIN. Plenty go in for the prize.

ANNA. Never too many enter.

ALVIN. Only one is first.

(*They face each other across the plant.* ALVIN *is* L *of it and* ANNA *is* R *of it*)

ANNA. The one that wins is all the others. They call it first but it's never there on its own. If it's by itself it's without a place altogether. It can only be first with the others.

ALVIN. But there has to be one best.

ANNA. The display is best. The green smell rising. Moving through the tents, pale and cool under the canvas wide above. Sunlight filters through. There's a shadow of haze and the plants almost suffocate with sweetness. Too much colour for one day. Too much for once. Like being abroad. (*She leans over the plant*) I see the petals. It should be out soon. You must have encouraged the sun when you washed the soot from the windows. We've had good weather for a month.

ALVIN (*picking up the shovel*) It's not just the weather that's brought it on. (*He moves to the box* LC) The old man's book has everything in it to do with it.

ANNA (*moving to* R *of Alvin*) I'm glad it's been helpful. (*She hands him the glove*)

ALVIN (*putting on the glove*) It says in the front that he was a vicar. (*He kneels at the box*)

ANNA. A Reverend, father, yes. The book was a present from one of his parishioners where we lived before we came here. She gave it to him on his retirement.

ALVIN (*taking some pieces of coal from the box and putting them in the shovel*) He doesn't talk like a churchman.

ANNA. What did you think he was?

D

ALVIN. Well, I'd imagined he'd been a representative or salesman like an insurance man. I mean, he doesn't seem like a vicar to me.

ANNA. If you'd known him long enough you'd think so.

ALVIN. It's the last thing I'd have suspected him of. He never speaks of it. He doesn't look like one, either.

ANNA. He tried to.

ALVIN (*rising*) He's like my dad and he hated churches. He said they weren't Christian. He looks like him a bit except my dad was younger and a lorry driver for a building firm.

ANNA. You don't look like a lorry driver's son.

ALVIN. You look like a vic . . . (*he pauses*) You look all right.

ANNA. I'll take the coal.

(ALVIN *puts the glove on top of the shovel and hands it to Anna, then hands her the torch.*

ANNA *exits up* C.

ALVIN *takes his plant and the ladder and follows Anna off up* C. *The lights* BLACK-OUT *to denote the passing of some weeks. After a few moments the lights come up on the Bowers' house* L.

ANNA *enters up* L, *goes into Jacob's bedroom, opens the window curtains, moves to the bedside table, pours and stirs the salts*)

Father. It's Tuesday. Father—Father . . . ? (*She stares at Jacob*)

(*The lights dim on the Bowers' house* L *and come up on the Hankers' house* R.

GEORGE *enters down* R.

MRS HANKER *is wheeled on in a chair down* R *by an* AMBULANCE MAN. *Her right arm and her neck are encased in plaster of paris so that her arm, supported by a brace and strut is held out and up in front of her at right angles, and she is wrapped in a blanket.* GEORGE *helps* MRS HANKER *out of the chair and into the hall. She leans on the newel post. The* AMBULANCE MAN *turns the chair to face* R. GEORGE *goes upstairs into Mrs Hanker's room and turns down the bed covers. The* AMBULANCE MAN *helps* MRS HANKER *up the stairs and into her room.* GEORGE *removes the blanket from* MRS HANKER *and the* AMBULANCE MAN *helps remove her dressing-gown.* MRS HANKER *gets into bed.*

The DOCTOR, *a nice enough general practitioner, enters* L *in the dim light and goes into the Bowers' living-room. He carries a small bag which he puts on the chair. He takes his stethoscope from the bag and goes upstairs to Jacob's room.* ANNA *meets him at the bedroom door and takes his hat. The* DOCTOR *goes to Jacob's bed and takes his pulse. He then uses his stethoscope. The* AMBULANCE MAN *goes on to the landing.* GEORGE *follows and hands him the blanket.*

The AMBULANCE MAN *then goes down the stairs and exits* R, *taking the wheel-chair with him. A clock chimes nine. The* DOCTOR *turns from the bed.* ANNA *looks at the* DOCTOR *who shakes his head*)

I knew he was.

(*The lights come up on the Bowers' house* L. ANNA *comes into the living-room and stands facing front. The* DOCTOR *draws the sheet over Jacob's face and pulls the screen around the bed.* GEORGE, *in the house* R, *comes downstairs, puts his coat on in the hall, then comes out of the front door and crosses to the Bowers' house* L. *The lights fade on the house* R. ANNA *turns to George*)

GEORGE. I'm sorry to bring you to the door when there's no post but I wanted to ask you if Alvin's out, if you'd ask him to call in at Calcutta Street to see his mother.

ANNA. He's gone to work.

GEORGE. I didn't think he'd be in. She's been asking, his mother, where I think he is and why he doesn't bother to visit. She says she doesn't care and doesn't want to see him and wouldn't talk to him if he came in and tried to, but I know she would. So could you ask him to call round on his own and not to say I asked him to, but pretend he comes of his own accord to see how she was?

ANNA. How is she?

GEORGE. Very well. I've looked after her and the neighbours have, too.

ANNA. What happened?

GEORGE. She broke her arm and her shoulder-blade, fractured her finger bone, was shocked and had injections then out she came in a bright red rash, her flesh blew up, all swollen with fluid she put on weight and got fat. She lies in bed, propped up waiting to be cared for. I do my best but she's not my responsibility.

(*The* DOCTOR *comes downstairs, removes his stethoscope and puts it in his bag*)

Good morning, Doctor.

DOCTOR. Mister Bland—good morning. How's Mrs Hanker?

GEORGE. I was just saying—she's very well.

(ANNA *moves down* L, *above the table*)

DOCTOR. I'll be in to see her on Thursday.

GEORGE. I'll tell her. Thank you. (*To Anna*) You will ask him to call for me?

ANNA. Yes.

GEORGE. Very much obliged. Thank you.

ANNA. Good-bye.

(GEORGE *exits up* L. *In the darkness he goes into his bedroom, removes his jacket, puts it over the back of the chair and sits on the bed*)

(*She turns to the Doctor*) What must I do?

(*The* DOCTOR *takes a box of tablets from his case and writes on the box*)

DOCTOR. Make yourself some tea, take one of these tablets every
D*

three hours to help you relax and I'll do the rest. The coroner will call and he'll arrange for the undertaker. Don't worry. (*He hands the box of tablets to Anna, closes his case and picks it up*)

ANNA. Thank you.

DOCTOR. Would you like me to inform any relatives?

ANNA (*handing him his hat*) No. There aren't many. I'll let them know after the funeral.

DOCTOR (*moving to R of Anna*) Chin up.

ANNA (*staring out front*) Of course.

(*The* DOCTOR *exits up* L. ANNA *picks up Jacob's magnifying glass from the table and puts it in the drawer. The lights fade on the house* L *and come up on the house* R. MRS HANKER *is propped up in bed. Her arm is still braced in front of her at right angles. She looks fat and rather horrible. She has sagged all over. She is turning the pages of a magazine with her good hand.*

ALVIN *enters down* R. *He wears a mackintosh. He goes into the hall.* GEORGE *rises, goes on to the landing and peers down into the hall*)

GEORGE. Alvin!

(ALVIN *goes up the stairs to the landing*)

(*He calls enthusiastically to Mrs Hanker*) You have a visitor, Ivy. (*To Alvin*) Let me take your coat, Alvin.

(GEORGE *helps* ALVIN *to remove his mackintosh, goes downstairs and hangs it in the hall.* ALVIN *goes slowly into Mrs Hanker's bedroom. He stands beside the bed, takes out a bag of sweets and puts it on the bed.* GEORGE *goes to his room, sits on his chair, takes out a cigarette, and lights it.* MRS HANKER *pushes the bag of sweets aside, ignores Alvin, and continues to turn the pages of her magazine.* ANNA, *in the dim light* L, *puts the pills on the sewing-table, takes an overall from the hall-stand, puts it on then goes into Jacob's room and closes the curtains. She stands above the screen, motionless, facing the bed with her left hand holding the top corner of the screen.*

JACOB, *concealed in the dim light and behind the screen, exits up* L)

ALVIN (*to Mrs Hanker*) Does it hurt?

(MRS HANKER *shakes her head*)

I'm living up Stroggen Hill Road, now. Old Mister Bower's house. (*He pauses*) He died this morning.

(MRS HANKER *turns a page*)

It looks as though it should be painful.

(MRS HANKER *turns a page*)

My plant that you saw's got some buds on it.

(MRS HANKER *reads*)

It's three feet tall, the stem.

(Mrs Hanker *turns a page*)

You're a lot fatter.

(Mrs Hanker *looks up at Alvin. Withdrawal, abstention and the misery these bring, on her face*)

Are you glad I came? Pleased to see me? I'm sorry I didn't come before.

(Mrs Hanker *turns a page*)

I'm sorry I threw water at you. I didn't mean you to get hurt.

(Mrs Hanker *turns a page*)

Don't you want to talk?

(Mrs Hanker *turns a few pages*)

I'll go, then. (*He moves to the door, pretending to leave*)

(George *rises and goes on to the landing*)

(*He returns to the bedside*) Would you like me to call often? (*He bends over and finds a way of getting past Mrs Hanker's arm to kiss her on the cheek*)

(Mrs Hanker *wipes the kiss away with a sharp move of her left hand.* Alvin *goes on to the landing and moves to the stairs*)

George (*intercepting* Alvin) Thank you for coming, Alvin.
Alvin. 'S all right.
George. I hung your coat up. (*He goes into his room and beckons to* Alvin)

(Alvin *follows George into his room.* George *offers Alvin a cigarette.* Alvin *refuses*)

You didn't tell her I asked you here, did you?
Alvin. No.
George. She's looking a lot better than she did a month back. I've done my best looking after her but she's not my responsibility, really, you know. We're not married. I'm not her husband. There was no oath for in sickness, health, richer, poorer, better or worse taken between us. We just fell in together for a while like. I never expected I'd have to look after her. I never wanted responsibility, just the good time of it was enough for me. Understand? (*He indicates for Alvin to sit on the bed*) Sit down, Alvin.

(Alvin *sits on the bed*)

(*He sits above Alvin on the bed*) I'm not the type for serious development or changes. I'm set in my ways. Always have been. I like things to stay as they are at the start. Besides it was all her doing. I've been cheated if you look at it. You can see I've been cheated. I'm a victim. She made the running. I'm involved unwillingly through her. I'm the innocent party. She's the injured one but I'm not to blame. I have to get out. That's why I want you to have this because I'm leaving next week. (*He picks up the white dressing-gown from the end of his bed and hands it to Alvin*) I never asked her to give it to me. (*He snaps his fingers and points to the back of the chair*) My coat. (*He rises*)

(ALVIN *rises and helps* GEORGE *to put on his coat*)

Next week the plaster comes off her arm and next week I go to Denbridge. I've got transferred to an indoor job. Registered parcels and express department.

ALVIN. I see.

GEORGE. I knew you'd understand, Alvin. You're a good lad. She'll soon be on her feet again. You can advertise for a lodger straight away. She'll perk up with you and a new lodger pottering about the house.

ALVIN. Yes.

GEORGE. Just one thing. I haven't told her yet. I didn't want to until I was sure you'd see things straight. So you'll let her know then, would you? Explain the position to her. I have to go to the club now. Darts and that.

ALVIN. Yes, I'll tell her, Mister Bland.

GEORGE. Good lad. (*He shakes hands with Alvin*) Good night.

(GEORGE *goes downstairs, heaves a sigh of relief, goes out of the front door and exits up* R. ALVIN *goes on to the landing, still holding the gown*)

MRS HANKER (*calling*) George. Are you there, George? Has he gone? Was that him banging the door, the dirty, snotty little runt. George.

(ALVIN *goes into Mrs Hanker's room, still holding the gown*)

Where's George?

ALVIN. Gone out.

MRS HANKER. What are you doing with that gown?

ALVIN. He gave it to me.

MRS HANKER. What for?

ALVIN. He's leaving next week. Got a job in Dembridge. He asked me to tell you.

MRS HANKER (*complacently*) He's not.

ALVIN. You have to advertise for a new lodger.

MRS HANKER. George wouldn't leave, he's not that sort.

ALVIN. He said your plaster comes off next week.

MRS HANKER. He can't leave. I need him. Anyhow, he's no right to push off, we're supposed to be in love.

ALVIN. He's gone to the club.

MRS HANKER. Don't tell me I've been wasting my time on him. Don't tell me *that* after all these months.

(ALVIN *goes abruptly on to the landing, and stands there, facing front and holding the dressing-gown. As Mrs Hanker calls, he makes a silent decision*)

(*She calls*) Alvin. Get him back here. Alvin. Fetch him. Alvin. Where are you? Go to the club, find him and fetch him.

(ALVIN *goes down the stairs, takes his coat from the hall-stand, and puts it on*)

He can't leave. I love him too much for that. He has to marry me. I won't be left. I can't be. He has to care. If I do he must. Somebody has to care as much as I do. Somebody has to care more than I know how. George. Alvin. Don't make me any more. I'm tired, worn out and away. Mrs Raistrick'll start knocking.

(ALVIN *goes out of the front door and exits down* R)

Come back. They've gone. I know when I'm alone. I can tell from past experience. I'll never get used to it, though. I'm damned if I'll ruddy get used to it. I'll have to cry like hell to remember how lonely I am. Nobody joins in with me for long if they can help it. Nobody joins me for long. (*She whimpers*)

(*The lights dim on the house* R *and come up on the house* L. ANNA *moves and opens the window curtains. She turns to the bed, collects the sheet, pillow and blankets, bundles them together, goes down the stairs and dumps them in the living-room. She returns to the bedroom, collects some of Jacob's clothing, including his clerical bib and collar, and a hot-water bottle.*

ALVIN, *carrying a suitcase, enters up* L *and stands at the Bowers' front door. As* ANNA *comes down the stairs, she looks at the suitcase, pauses an instant, then goes briskly to the pile of bedding and drops the other things beside it*)

ALVIN. I *have* to go and look after her.

(ANNA *picks up the pillow and removes the pillow-slip*)

ANNA. You won't be coming back, then? (*She puts the pillow on the chair* R)

ALVIN (*standing his suitcase in the hall*) She's hurt, very hurt. It's awful to see her.

ANNA. I shall miss your plant. (*She folds the pillow-slip and puts it on the chair*)

ALVIN. Can't I leave it in the greenhouse?

ANNA (*picking up the sheet and folding it*) I don't want it. If you do, take it. I'd only throw it in the dustbin. (*She puts the sheet on the chair*)

ALVIN. Why?

ANNA. To avoid remembering, I suppose. (*She picks up a blanket and starts to fold it*)

ALVIN. I should take it then, if you'd throw it away.

ANNA. Yes, take it. (*She drops the blanket, goes upstairs, takes a shoe-*

*box from under the bedside table and noisily puts all Jacob's medicine bottles
from the table into it*)

ALVIN *collects a second coat from the hall-stand and puts it over his arm.*
ANNA *comes downstairs with the shoe-box and puts it on the sewing-table*)

ALVIN. I'm sorry you won't remember.

(ANNA *puts the box of tablets into the shoe-box*)

ANNA. Aren't you going to take your games and things? (*She
picks up the blanket, folds it and puts it on the chair* R)

ALVIN. I thought they could go to the White Elephant Stall at the
Flower Show.

ANNA. All right. I'll see to it.

ALVIN. Thank you. Do you want me to come back and stay with
you tonight?

ANNA. No.

ALVIN (*picking up his suitcase*) You won't mind being in the house
alone?

ANNA (*picking up the clothes and putting them on the chair* R) It won't
make any difference with him gone. He was old.

ALVIN. I see.

(ANNA *picks up the hot-water bottle and puts it on the chair* L)

Shall I come with you to the funeral?

ANNA. No. I lived with him. I'll bury him. (*She picks up Jacob's
clerical bib, folds it and puts it on the chair* R)

ALVIN. Yes, all right, if you like. I'm sorry.

(ANNA *picks up the second blanket.*

ALVIN *exits up* L. ANNA *hesitates for a moment whilst holding the
blanket with outstretched arms. She finishes folding it and places it on the
chair* R. *The lights dim on the house* L *and come up on the house* R.

ALVIN *enters up* C, *carrying the coat and suitcase. He goes into the
kitchen, then the hall, and picks up the dressing-gown from the hall-table.
He goes upstairs into his room, dumps the suitcase on the floor and the coat
on the chair. He hangs the gown behind the door, looks around, closes the
door, comes downstairs and exits down* R. ANNA, *meanwhile, in the dim
light, goes upstairs, collects Jacob's walking-stick, dressing-gown and
Bible, comes downstairs, puts the gown over the back of the chair* L, *the
Bible on the chair* R *and lays the stick across the chair* L. *She goes to the hall-
stand, takes down a raincoat with a mourning band on one arm, and a black
headscarf. She goes to the chair* R, *puts the scarf on the chair, and puts on
her raincoat. As she does so, faint nondescript organ music is heard.*

ANNA *puts on her headscarf, picks up the Bible and exits up* L. *The
lights on the houses* R *and* L *fade, and come up on the forestage* LC. *The box
is now Jacob's grave.*

ALVIN *enters down* R. *He enters backwards and turns. He is carrying
the lily, now in full bloom.*

ANNA *enters down* L. *They meet at Jacob's grave.* ALVIN *stands* R *of the box and* ANNA *is* L *of it*)

Aren't you going to get him a headstone?

ANNA. I've ordered one.

ALVIN. Oh, yes?

ANNA. How's your mother?

ALVIN. All right.

ANNA. I hear we're going to have a new postman next week.

ALVIN. Yes. Mister Bland's going to Denbridge to work.

ANNA. They called round this morning about those things of yours. The games and things.

ALVIN. They'll sell them easily, don't you think?

ANNA. Oh, yes, I'm sure.

ALVIN. It's a nice day.

ANNA. Oh, yes.

ALVIN. Shall we walk up Stroggen Hill?

ANNA. Why not? Stop off on the way back and I'll make tea.

ALVIN. All right. (*He puts the plant on the grave and steps back*)

ANNA. It's lovely now, isn't it?

ALVIN. Yes. It's all right.

The organ music swells as the CURTAIN *starts to fall, and the lights dim to* BLACK-OUT, *except for a spotlight focused on the plant. The plant is left on the box in front of the* CURTAIN. *The light fades from it after the* CURTAIN *is down, leaving only the organ music playing.*

CURTAIN

FURNITURE AND PROPERTY LIST

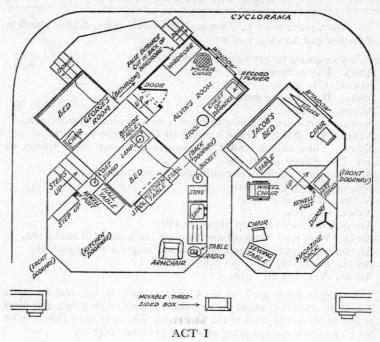

MOVABLE THREE-SIDED BOX →

ACT I

BOWERS' HOUSE L

On stage:

In Jacobs' room: Bed with mattress, 2 blankets, pillow, sheet
              Dressing-gown and slippers
              Walking-stick (hung on bed)
              Screen
              Window curtains
              Chair
              Bedside table. *On it:* Bible, jug of water, medicine bottles, pill boxes, glass, spoon, tin of Andrews salts

In living-room: Magazine rack. *In it:* magazines and newspapers
              Sewing-table
              In drawers: bottle of ink, pen, writing-paper, envelopes, magnifying glass, torch, box of pins
              On it: vase of dead Michaelmas daisies
              Upright chair
              Wheel-chair. *On it:* blanket
              Dressmaker's dummy. *On it:* dress

In hall: hall-stand. *On it:* Anna's raincoat, scarf, beret and overall

HANKERS' HOUSE R

On landing: runner

In kitchen: garbage bucket. *In it:* garbage
gas stove. *On plate-rack:* pot of tea, clean plate, dish-
cloth, clock
sink. *In it:* bowl of water, plates, etc., for washing,
mop
draining-board. *On it:* cup, saucer, mug, cutlery for
washing
cupboard under draining-board. *In it:* plate with
slices ham, plate of bread and butter
table (down L) *On it:* radio, ashtray
armchair. *On it:* newspaper
Under it: George's slippers
table (R) *On it:* bowl of cornflakes, dessert spoon,
plate with bread and butter, sugar, mug, teaspoon, sandwich box, thermos flask, cruet
2 stools

In hall: table. *Under it:* shopping basket with Mrs Hanker's
handbag
coat-stand. *On it:* Alvin's jacket, balaclava and scarf;
Mrs Hanker's coat and scarf
Under it: Alvin's wellingtons and shoes
Outside front door: dustbin, bottle of milk

In George's room: bed and bedding. *In it:* pyjamas
alarm clock
George's slippers
Chair. *On it:* George's shirt

In Mrs Hanker's room: bed and bedding
bedside table. *On it:* table-lamp

In Alvin's room: wardrobe. *In it:* clothing, plant
On it: books, papers, comics, garden-
ing books
chest of drawers. *On it:* record-player, records
Under it: box with plant bulb
and bag of sand; shoe-box,
bottle of water
wicker chair
stool
hanging behind door: overalls, white towelling
dressing-gown
key in door
window curtains
Box on forestage LC. *In it:* earth and coal

Off stage: Bicycle with lamp (GEORGE)
  Packet of letters with postcard, registered letter and air mail letter (GEORGE)
  Postbag (GEORGE)
  Pencil (GEORGE)
  Registration receipt (GEORGE)
  Tray. *On it:* napkin in ring, plate with bread and butter, egg in egg-cup, egg spoon, knife, pot of tea, milk, sugar, cup, saucer and teaspoon (ANNA)
  Towel (GEORGE)

ACT II

BOWERS' HOUSE

Strike: Dead Michaelmas daisies
  Breakfast tray
  Writing materials
  Dress from dummy

Set: *On chair:* Anna's cardigan
  Fresh daisies in vase

HANKERS' HOUSE

Strike: Kitchen clock
  Everything except cruet from kitchen table
  George's hat and jacket

Set: *On kitchen chair:* newspaper
  Rubbish in garbage bucket
  Vacuum flask on stove
  Sandwich box on table
  Outside front door: bottle of milk
  On kitchen table: bowl of cornflakes, dessert spoon, plate for breaking, knife, plate with bread and butter
  In cupboard under draining-board: ladling can and wash leather

Off stage: Bicycle (GEORGE)
  Tray. *On it:* 2 mugs of Horlicks, tin of Horlicks (MRS HANKER)
  Library book for tickets (ANNA)
  Groceries for shopping (MRS HANKER)
  Plant (ALVIN)
  Ladder (GEORGE)

Personal: ANNA: handbag
  GEORGE: cigarettes, matches

ACT III

BOWERS' HOUSE

Strike: Vase with daisies
        Plant
        Library book
        Magazine rack

Set: Sewing-table (L) *On it:* snakes and ladders game, magnifying glass
                      In it: torch
      Upright chair and wheel-chair above table
      Upright chair (R) *On it:* knitting, knitting-bag, pattern
      On wheel-chair: walking-stick
      On hall-stand: Anna's raincoat with black mourning band, black head-
        scarf, Alvin's coat
      Under Jacob's bed: shoe-box
      In Jacob's bed: Jacob's clothing, clerical collar and bib, hot-water
        bottle

HANKERS' HOUSE

Strike: Everything from kitchen table
        Pieces of broken plate
        Milk bottles
        Horlicks, mugs and tray
        Record-player and records

Set: *On George's bed:* white dressing-gown
      On Mrs Hanker's bed: magazine
      In Alvin's room: stool on wardrobe
Tidy rooms generally

Off stage: Suitcase (ALVIN)
           Bag of sweets (ALVIN)
           Wheel-chair and blanket (AMBULANCE MAN)
           Bandages and arm support (MRS HANKER)
           Medical bag. *In it:* stethoscope, box of pills (DOCTOR)
           Stepladder with thermometer and plant (ALVIN)
           Lily in full bloom (ALVIN)
           Coal shovel and glove (ANNA)

Personal: DOCTOR: pencil
          GEORGE: cigarettes, matches

LIGHTING PLOT

Property fittings required: 4 shaded pendants, 1 table-lamp

Interior. A composite setting of two houses, the house R having four
rooms and the house L, two rooms. The same setting throughout

THE MAIN ACTING AREAS are in the four rooms R, the two rooms L,
and three areas of the forestage, RC, C and LC

THE APPARENT SOURCES OF LIGHT are four shaded pendants R, RC, C
LC, a table-lamp RC, and windows up C and up LC

ACT I. Morning

To open: The stage in darkness
          Daylight outside windows

Cue 1	After rise of CURTAIN	(Page 2)
	Bring up light on George's room R	
Cue 2	GEORGE exits	(Page 2)
	Fade lights on George's room	
	Bring lights up on living-room L	
Cue 3	ANNA opens window curtains	(Page 2)
	Bring up lights on Jacob's room L	
Cue 4	ANNA sits at window	(Page 3)
	Dim lights on living-room L and Jacob's room L	
	Bring up lights on kitchen and Alvin's room R	
Cue 5	ALVIN leaves his room	(Page 3)
	Fade lights on Alvin's room	
Cue 6	MRS HANKER goes to George's room	(Page 8)
	Bring up lights on George's room	
Cue 7	GEORGE: ". . . should wear goloshes."	(Page 9)
	Dim lights on house R	
	Bring up lights on house L	
Cue 8	MRS HANKER exits R	(Page 9)
	Fade lights on house R	
Cue 9	JACOB comes downstairs	(Page 9)
	Fade light on Jacob's room	
Cue 10	JACOB: ". . . Flower Show already, Anna."	(Page 12)
	Fade lights on house L	
	Bring up lights on house R	
Cue 11	MRS HANKER: "Two and fourpence."	(Page 17)
	Fade lights in kitchen R	

Cue 12	ALVIN: "I haven't."	(Page 19)
	Bring up lights on kitchen	
Cue 13	ALVIN puts on scarf and balaclava	(Page 21)
	Bring up lights on house L	
Cue 14	MRS HANKER: "Lovely."	(Page 22)
	Fade lights on house R	
Cue 15	ANNA leaves house	(Page 23)
	Fade lights on house L	
	Bring up lights down L *and down* R	

ACT II. Night

To open: Stage in darkness

Cue 16	After rise of CURTAIN	(Page 24)
	Bring up lights down LC	
Cue 17	ALVIN and ANNA exit up C	(Page 26)
	Fade lights down LC	
	Bring up lights down L	
Cue 18	ANNA stops, turns and looks after Alvin	(Page 27)
	BLACK-OUT	
Cue 19	ANNA exits	(Page 27)
	Bring up lights on kitchen R	
Cue 20	GEORGE goes to his room	(Page 27)
	Bring up lights on George's room	
Cue 21	MRS HANKER: ". . . peace of a night-time."	(Page 28)
	Fade lights on kitchen R	
Cue 22	MRS HANKER switches on lamp	(Page 28)
	Bring up light on Mrs Hanker's room	
Cue 23	MRS HANKER switches out lamp	(Page 28)
	Fade lights on Mrs Hanker's and George's rooms	
Cue 24	MRS HANKER switches on lamp	(Page 29)
	Bring up lights on Mrs Hanker's room	
Cue 25	GEORGE gets out of bed	(Page 29)
	Bring up lights on George's room	
Cue 26	MRS HANKER switches off lamp	(Page 31)
	Fade lights on Mrs Hanker's room	
Cue 27	MRS HANKER removes pyjama jacket	(Page 31)
	BLACK-OUT	
Cue 28	Follows above cue	(Page 31)
	Bring up lights on Alvin's room	
Cue 29	ALVIN opens wardrobe	(Page 33)
	BLACK-OUT *for a few moments*	

Cue 30	ALVIN takes plant from wardrobe *Bring up lights on kitchen* R	(Page 33)
Cue 31	MRS HANKER: ". . . care a damn." *Fade lights on kitchen*	(Page 35)
Cue 32	Follows above cue *Bring up lights on kitchen and Alvin's room*	(Page 35)
Cue 33	MRS HANKER exits *Fade lights on kitchen* *Bring up lights on forestage*	(Page 36)
Cue 34	ANNA and ALVIN exit L *Fade lights on forestage* *Bring up lights on kitchen*	(Page 38)
Cue 35	GEORGE exits *Fade lights on house* R *Bring up lights on living-room* L	(Page 41)

ACT III.   Evening

To open:	The stage in darkness	
Cue 36	After rise of CURTAIN *Bring up lights on house* L	(Page 42)
Cue 37	ANNA exits up L *Fade lights on house* L *Bring up lights on forestage area* C	(Page 44)
Cue 38	ANNA and ALVIN exit BLACK-OUT	(Page 46)
Cue 39	Follows above cue *Bring up lights on house* L	(Page 46)
Cue 40	ANNA: "Father . . . ?" *Dim lights on house* L *Bring up lights on house* R	(Page 46)
Cue 41	ANNA: "I knew he was." *Bring up lights on house* L	(Page 46)
Cue 42	GEORGE leaves the house R *Fade lights on house* R	(Page 47)
Cue 43	ANNA puts magnifying glass in drawer *Fade lights on house* L *Bring up lights on house* R	(Page 48)
Cue 44	MRS HANKER: ". . . me for long." *Fade lights on house* R *Bring up lights on house* L	(Page 51)

Cue 45   ANNA places second blanket on chair R   (Page 52)
              Dim lights on house L
              Bring up lights on house R

Cue 46   ANNA exits   (Page 52)
              Fade lights on houses R *and* L
              Bring up lights on forestage LC

Cue 47   As CURTAIN falls   (Page 53)
              BLACK-OUT *except for a spotlight on plant* LC

Cue 48   After fall of CURTAIN   (Page 53)
              Take out spotlight

EFFECTS PLOT

ACT I

Cue 1	At rise of CURTAIN *Sound of clock ticking*	(Page 2)
Cue 2	After rise of CURTAIN *Alarm clock rings*	(Page 2)
Cue 3	GEORGE hits clock for second time *Alarm stops*	(Page 2)
Cue 4	GEORGE exits *Stop clock ticking*	(Page 2)
Cue 5	ANNA: "Yes, Wednesday." *A clock chimes the half-hour*	(Page 3)
Cue 6	The lights comeup on the kitchen *Music from radio "Fascination"*	(Page 3)
Cue 7	ANNA: ". . . exciting has happened." *Clock strikes five*	(Page 10)
Cue 8	ALVIN switches on record-player *Music from record-player*	(Page 14)
Cue 9	ALVIN adjusts record-player *Increase volume of music*	(Page 15)
Cue 10	ALVIN adjusts record-player *Reduce volume of music*	(Page 15)
Cue 11	ALVIN adjusts record-player *Increase volume of music*	(Page 16)
Cue 12	ALVIN lifts pick-up *Stop music*	(Page 16)

ACT II

Cue 13	ALVIN: "They're in Latin." *Torch flashes*	(Page 25)
Cue 14	GEORGE winds alarm clock *Sound of clock ticking. This continues throughout the scene*	(Page 28)
Cue 15	The lights come up on the kitchen *Music from the radio "La Mer"*	(Page 33)

Cue 16 Mrs Hanker falls from window   (Page 40)
       Sound of crash

Cue 17 Alvin throws can out of window   (Page 40)
       Sound of clatter

ACT III

Cue 18 The Ambulance Man exits   (Page 46)
       A clock chimes nine

Cue 19 Anna puts on coat   (Page 52)
       Sound of organ music

Cue 20 Alvin: "It's all right."   (Page 53)
       Organ music swells

MADE AND PRINTED IN GREAT BRITAIN BY
LATIMER TREND AND CO. LTD, PLYMOUTH
MADE IN ENGLAND